First World War
and Army of Occupation
War Diary
France, Belgium and Germany

4 DIVISION
12 Infantry Brigade,
Brigade Machine Gun Company
24 January 1916 - 11 January 1918

WO95/1509/1

The Naval & Military Press Ltd
www.nmarchive.com
Published in association with The National Archives

Published by

The Naval & Military Press Ltd

Unit 10 Ridgewood Industrial Park,

Uckfield, East Sussex,

TN22 5QE England

Tel: +44 (0) 1825 749494

www.naval-military-press.com

www.nmarchive.com

This diary has been reprinted in facsimile from the original. Any imperfections are inevitably reproduced and the quality may fall short of modern type and cartographic standards.

© **Crown Copyright**
Images reproduced by permission of The National Archives, London, England, 2015.

Contents

Document type	Place/Title	Date From	Date To
Heading	WO95/1509/1 4 Divn. 12 Inf. Brigade Brig M/Gun Co. 1916 Jan-1918 Jan		
Heading	12 Infantry Brigade. Bde Machine Gun Coy. 1916 Jan To 1918 Jan Bde Trench Mortar Bty 1916 Jan To 1918 Apr.		
Heading	12th Brigade Machine Gun Company January To June 1916		
Heading	War Diary of No. 12 Company Machine Gun Corps. From January 24th 1916 To June 30th 1916 Volume I With Appendices		
War Diary	Ailly Le Haut Clocher	24/01/1916	31/01/1916
War Diary	Halloy	01/02/1916	01/02/1916
War Diary	Puschvillers	02/02/1916	02/02/1916
War Diary	Acheux	03/02/1916	05/02/1916
War Diary	Mailly-Maillet	06/02/1916	10/02/1916
War Diary	Colincamps	10/02/1916	03/03/1916
War Diary	Sailly-Au-Bois	04/03/1916	04/03/1916
War Diary	Halloy	05/03/1916	05/03/1916
War Diary	Bouquemaison	06/03/1916	09/03/1916
War Diary	Barly	10/03/1916	17/03/1916
War Diary	Halloy	18/03/1916	18/03/1916
War Diary	Bailleulval	19/03/1916	01/05/1916
War Diary	Le Sovich	02/05/1916	07/05/1916
War Diary	Bertrancourt	08/05/1916	23/05/1916
War Diary	Gorges	23/05/1916	25/05/1916
War Diary	Cumont Farm	26/05/1916	09/06/1916
War Diary	Gorges	10/06/1916	10/06/1916
War Diary	Beauval	11/06/1916	11/06/1916
War Diary	Authie	12/06/1916	14/06/1916
War Diary	Bertrancourt	15/06/1916	30/06/1916
Miscellaneous	12th Brigade Defence Scheme Colincamps Sector		
Miscellaneous	Defence 12th Brigade B.M.N. Scheme		
War Diary	Objectives Of 4th Division		
War Diary	Order Of 1st Assembly Of 12th Bde		
War Diary	Order Of 2nd Assembly Of 12th Brigade.		
War Diary	The Attack Order Of		
War Diary	Para (1)		
Miscellaneous	Position Of Brigade During Advance		
Heading	4th Division War Diaries 12th Infantry Bde M.G. Coy. Formed 24-1-16 January To August 1916		
Heading	4th Division War Diaries 12th Infantry Bde M.G. Coy. Formed 24-1-16 January To August 1916 January 1918		
Heading	War Diary of No. 12 Machine Gun Company Machine Gun Corps From July 1st 1916 To July 31st 1916 Volume I Appendices 6 & 7		
War Diary	Trenches In Front Of Serre	01/07/1918	01/07/1918
War Diary	Trenches	01/07/1916	02/07/1916
War Diary	Trenches Of Sucrerie Maily Maillet	03/07/1916	05/07/1916
War Diary	Mailly-Maillet And Trenches.	06/07/1916	10/07/1916
War Diary	Bertrancourt	11/07/1916	17/07/1916

War Diary	Camp At P17b And Trenches	17/07/1916	21/07/1916
War Diary	Vauchelles-Les-Authie	21/07/1916	23/07/1916
War Diary	Farm At D18b3.7	23/07/1916	24/07/1916
War Diary	Farm At D18b3.7 Near Houtkerque	25/07/1916	27/07/1916
War Diary	Camp At A22d 7.3	28/07/1916	28/07/1916
War Diary	Camp At A22d 7.3	29/07/1916	31/07/1916
Heading	12th Brigade 4th Division 12th Infantry Brigade Machine Gun Company August 1916		
War Diary	Camp At A22d 7.3	01/08/1916	03/08/1916
War Diary	Yser Canal Bank At C25a 5.5 (Yperlee)	04/08/1916	20/08/1916
War Diary	Poperinghe	21/08/1916	23/08/1916
War Diary	Dugout On Comines-Ypres Canal At I25c	24/08/1916	25/08/1916
War Diary	Trenches Coy H.Q. Of I25c On Ypres-comines Canal	26/08/1916	26/08/1916
War Diary	Trenches	26/08/1916	31/08/1916
Heading	4th Division War Diaries 12th Infantry Bde M.G. Coy. September To December 1916		
Heading	12th Brigade 4th Division 12th Infantry Brigade Machine Gun Company September 1916		
War Diary	Houtpoutre Siding Near Poperinghe	17/09/1916	22/09/1916
War Diary	Trenches	01/09/1916	08/09/1916
War Diary	Poperinghe	09/09/1916	16/09/1916
War Diary	Rainneville	23/09/1916	25/09/1916
War Diary	Allonville	25/09/1916	26/09/1916
War Diary	La Neuville	27/09/1916	30/09/1916
Heading	12th Brigade 4th Division 12th Infantry Brigade Machine Gun Company October 1916		
War Diary	La Neuville	01/10/1916	08/10/1916
War Diary	Citadel-Camp	08/10/1916	12/10/1916
War Diary	Trenches	12/10/1916	31/10/1916
Miscellaneous	12th Infantry Brigade N.G.R. 263		
Miscellaneous	12th Machine Gun Company Copy Of Final Report On Co-operation Of No 12 Machine Gun Company Operation Of 12th Oct 1916 By Lieut. W.E. Roberton Commanding 12th Machine Gun Company Appendix I A	12/10/1916	12/10/1916
Miscellaneous	12th Machine Gun Company-Opertions 18th Oct By Lieut. W.E. Roberton Comdg No. 12 Machine Gun Company Sent To No.12 Inf Brigde 19th Oct Appendix II B	18/10/1916	18/10/1916
Operation(al) Order(s)	Report On Operation 23rd Oct Appendix III A	23/10/1916	23/10/1916
Operation(al) Order(s)	Copy Of Final Report On Operation 23rd Oct Sent To No 12 Inf Brigade. By Lieut. W.W. Roberton. Comdg No. 12 Machine Gun Company Appendix III B	23/10/1916	23/10/1916
Miscellaneous	Remarks, Criticism And Suggestions Category (e) Bde. G.R. 63 By Lieut. W.E. Roberton Comdg No. 12 Machine Gun Company Appendix IV		
Heading	12th Brigade 4th Division 12th Infantry Brigade Machine Gun Company November 1916		
War Diary	Woirel	01/11/1916	03/11/1916
War Diary	Le Plouy	04/11/1916	30/11/1916
Heading	12th Brigade 4th Division 12th Infantry Brigade Machine Gun Company December 1916		
Heading	War Diary of 12th Machine Gun Company From 1st December 1916 To 31st December 1916 Volume 12		
War Diary	Le Plouy	01/12/1916	03/12/1916
War Diary	Camp 107 N.E. Of Bray-Sur-Somme	03/12/1916	04/12/1916

War Diary	Camp E. Of Bronfay FM.	04/12/1916	05/12/1916
War Diary	Maricourt Camp (A.16.d. 3.3)	06/12/1916	06/12/1916
War Diary	Trenches	07/12/1916	26/12/1916
War Diary	Camp 16 (F.30. A.G.I.)	27/12/1916	28/12/1916
War Diary	Bailly-Laurette	29/12/1916	31/12/1916
Operation(al) Order(s)	12th Infantry Brigade Operation Order No. 56 Appendix A	05/12/1916	05/12/1916
Miscellaneous	Relief Order By Captain J.B. Baber M.C. Commanding 12th Machine Gun Company Appendix B		
Heading	4th Division 12th Infantry Bde 12th M.G.C. January To December 1917		
Heading	War Diary of 12th Machine Gun Company From 1st January 1917 To 31st January 1917 Volume 13		
War Diary	Sailly-Laurette	01/01/1917	23/01/1917
War Diary	Bray	24/01/1917	24/01/1917
War Diary	Suzanne	25/01/1917	31/01/1917
Operation(al) Order(s)	No. 12 Machine Gun Company Operation Order No. 1	22/01/1917	22/01/1917
Operation(al) Order(s)	No. 12 Machine Gun Company Operation Order No. 2	23/01/1917	23/01/1917
Miscellaneous	Amendment To No. 12 Machine Gun Company Operation Order No. 22	23/01/1917	23/01/1917
Operation(al) Order(s)	No 12 Machine Gun Company Operation Order No. 3	30/01/1917	30/01/1917
Heading	War Diary of No. 12 Machine Gun Company From 1st February 1917 To 29th February 1917 (Volume 12)		
War Diary	Suzanne	01/02/1917	01/02/1917
War Diary	Curlu	01/02/1917	01/02/1917
War Diary	Junction Wood Marrieres Wood	01/02/1917	03/02/1917
War Diary	Marrieres Wood	04/02/1917	19/02/1917
War Diary	Loiter Camp	20/02/1917	20/02/1917
War Diary	Camp 117	21/02/1917	21/02/1917
War Diary	Corbie	22/02/1917	28/02/1917
Heading	War Diary of No 12 Machine Gun Company From 1st March 1917 To 31st March 1917 (Volumne XV)		
War Diary	Corbie	01/03/1917	04/03/1917
War Diary	Montonvillers	05/03/1917	05/03/1917
War Diary	Beauval	06/03/1917	06/03/1917
War Diary	Noeux	07/03/1917	07/03/1917
War Diary	Boufflers	08/03/1917	22/03/1917
War Diary	Auxi-Le-Chateau	22/03/1917	22/03/1917
War Diary	Chelers	22/03/1917	22/03/1917
War Diary	Magnicourt	22/03/1917	22/03/1917
War Diary	E Coivres	22/03/1917	23/03/1917
War Diary	Boufflers	24/03/1917	24/03/1917
War Diary	Magnicourt	25/03/1917	31/03/1917
Heading	War Diary of No. 12 Machine Gun Company From 1st April 1917 To 30th April 1917 (Volumne 14)		
War Diary	Magnicourt	01/04/1917	07/04/1917
War Diary	V Camp 1000 Yds East Of Etrun	08/04/1917	08/04/1917
War Diary	V Camp	09/04/1917	09/04/1917
War Diary	G. II	09/04/1917	09/04/1917
War Diary	Athies	10/04/1917	10/04/1917
War Diary	Hive	10/04/1917	14/04/1917
War Diary	G. II	15/04/1917	20/04/1917
War Diary	Montenescourt	20/04/1917	21/04/1917
War Diary	Manin	21/04/1917	22/04/1917
War Diary	Beaufort	22/04/1917	23/04/1917
War Diary	Le Cauroy	23/04/1917	24/04/1917

War Diary	Sars Le Bois	26/04/1917	28/04/1917
War Diary	Tilloy Les Hermaville	28/04/1917	29/04/1917
War Diary	G. II	29/04/1917	30/04/1917
Heading	War Diary of No. 12 Machine Gun Company From 1st May 1917 To 31st May 1917 (Volumne XVII)		
War Diary	H 22b	01/05/1917	02/05/1917
War Diary	Fampoux	03/05/1917	12/05/1917
War Diary	G 17	12/05/1917	13/05/1917
War Diary	Penin	13/04/1917	31/05/1917
Heading	War Diary of No. 12 Machine Gun Company From 1st June 1917 To 30th June 1917 (Volumne 18)		
War Diary	Penin	01/06/1917	08/06/1917
War Diary	Doffine Farm	08/06/1917	08/06/1917
War Diary	Penin	09/06/1917	09/06/1917
War Diary	Arras	10/06/1917	10/06/1917
War Diary	Hive	11/06/1917	12/06/1917
War Diary	Front Line	13/06/1917	16/06/1917
War Diary	Les The Hive	16/06/1917	18/06/1917
War Diary	Fife Camp	18/06/1917	27/06/1917
War Diary	Fife Camp H 35d 5.9	27/06/1917	30/06/1917
Heading	War Diary of No. 12 Machine Gun Company From 1st July 1917 To 31st July 1917 (Volumne XIX)		
War Diary	H. 35d. 5.9	01/07/1917	13/07/1917
War Diary	Fife Camp	13/07/1917	16/07/1917
War Diary	G 24c 9.1	16/07/1917	31/07/1917
Heading	War Diary of No 12 Machine Gun Company From 1st August 1947 To 31st August 1917 (Volumne XVIII)		
War Diary	Trenches Monchy Sector	01/08/1917	02/08/1917
War Diary	Trenches Monchy Area	02/08/1917	13/08/1917
War Diary	Dingwall Camp	14/08/1917	29/08/1917
War Diary	Trenches Moncy Area	30/08/1917	31/08/1917
Heading	War Diary of No 12 Machine Gun Company From 1st September 1917 To 31st September 1917		
War Diary	Trenches Monchy Area	01/09/1917	07/09/1917
War Diary	Arras	08/09/1917	08/09/1917
War Diary	Blaireville Camp No.2	08/09/1917	19/09/1917
War Diary	Peselhoek	19/09/1917	19/09/1917
War Diary	Saskatoon Camp	19/09/1917	27/09/1917
War Diary	Woolf Camp	27/09/1917	27/09/1917
War Diary	Trenches	27/09/1917	29/09/1917
War Diary	Trenches Langemarck Area	30/09/1917	30/09/1917
Heading	War Diary of No. 12 Machine Gun Company From 1st October 1917 To 31st October 1917 (Volume XXII)		
War Diary	Trenches	01/10/1917	03/10/1917
War Diary	Solferino Camp	03/10/1917	07/10/1917
War Diary	Line	08/10/1917	15/10/1917
War Diary	Point Camp	15/10/1917	16/10/1917
War Diary	St-Jan-Der-Diexen	16/10/1917	18/10/1917
War Diary	Aubigny	19/10/1917	19/10/1917
War Diary	Noyelette	20/10/1917	24/10/1917
War Diary	Arras	25/10/1917	31/10/1917
Heading	War Diary of No. 12 Machine Gun Company From 1st November 1917 To 30th November 1917 (Volume XXLII)		
War Diary	Arras	01/11/1917	07/11/1917
War Diary	Line N 4b 9048	08/11/1917	23/11/1917

War Diary	Arras	23/11/1917	30/11/1917
Heading	War Diary of 12th Machine Gun Company From 1st December 1917 To 31st December 1917 (Volume XXIV)		
War Diary	Arras	01/12/1917	03/12/1917
War Diary	Line Monchy Right Sub-Sector	03/12/1917	19/12/1917
War Diary	Arras	20/12/1917	26/12/1917
War Diary	Line Monchy Left-Sub-Sector	27/12/1917	31/12/1917
Operation(al) Order(s)	No. 12 Machine Gun Company Operation Order No. 30 Appendix "A"	01/12/1917	01/12/1917
Operation(al) Order(s)	No. 12 Machine Gun Company Operation Order No. 31 Appendix "B"	19/12/1917	19/12/1917
Operation(al) Order(s)	1st Machine Gun Company Operation Order No. 32 Appendix "C"	26/12/1917	26/12/1917
Heading	4th Division 12th M.G.C. January 1918		
Heading	War Diary of 12th Machine Gun Company From 1st January 1918 To 31st January 1918 (Volume XXV)		
War Diary	Line Monchy Left Sub-Sector	01/01/1918	12/01/1918
War Diary	Bois-Des-Boeuffs	13/01/1918	20/01/1918
War Diary	Line Monchy Right Sub-Sector	21/01/1918	31/01/1918
Operation(al) Order(s)	12th Machine Gun Company Operation Order No. 25 Appendix "A"	19/01/1918	19/01/1918
War Diary	12th Machine Gun Company Operation Order No. 25 Appendix "B"	11/01/1918	11/01/1918

WO 95 1609/1

4 DIVN.
12 INF. BRIGADE
BRIG. M/GUN CO. 1916 JAN — 1918 JAN

12 INFANTRY BRIGADE.

BDE MACHINE GUN COY.
1916 JAN TO 1918 JAN.

BDE TRENCH MORTAR BTY
1916 JAN TO 1918 APR.

1509

12th Brigade.

4th Division.

Company formed 24th January 1916

12th Brigade

MACHINE GUN COMPANY

JANUARY TO JUNE 1916

Vol I To 6

CONFIDENTIAL.

WAR DIARY

of

No. 12 Company Machine Gun Corps.

from January 24th 1916 to June 30th 1916

VOLUME I with appendices.

Army Form C. 2118.

WAR DIARY
or
INTELLIGENCE SUMMARY.
(Erase heading not required.)

Instructions regarding War Diaries and Intelligence Summaries are contained in F. S. Regs., Part II. and the Staff Manual respectively. Title pages will be prepared in manuscript.

Place	Date	Hour	Summary of Events and Information	Remarks and references to Appendices
AILLY LE HAUT CLOCHER	Jany 1916 24th		The company, less one complete section formed, complete section being furnished by the machine gun sections of the units of the 12th Brigade viz:— 1st Kings Own Royal Lancaster Regt, 2nd Lancashire Fusiliers and 2nd Essex Regt. Capt G.B. SLEIGH Brigade machine gun officer assumed Command of the Company and the following officers also joined Lt A.K. BOYD 2nd Lt E. ROGERS from 2nd Lancashire Fusiliers Lt J. LIGHTBODY from the 1st Kings Own Regt and Lt R.M. STRAIGHT from 2nd Essex.	
	25th 27th		Company being rearranged and organized	9p
	28th		Lt K.R.G. BROWNE from 2nd Essex Regt joined the Company.	1t
	29th 31st Feb 1st		Company training and organizing	1t
HALLOY	2nd		The company moved to HALLOY.	7p
PUSCHVILLERS	3rd		The Company moved to PUSCHVILLERS. Move to ACHEUX. Lt R.C. STONE from 1st Kings Own Regt. joined the	1t
ACHEUX	4th		Company Machine gun positions held by the 10th Brigade Machine Gun company in the line in front of COLINCAMPS were reconnoitred by officers.	9p

WAR DIARY or INTELLIGENCE SUMMARY

Army Form C. 2118.

Place	Date	Hour	Summary of Events and Information	Remarks and references to Appendices
ACHEUX	Feb 5th		The company relieved the 10th Brigade Company in the line. Headquarters of the Company here at MAILLY-MAILLET. The remaining section to complete the strength was lent temporarily by the 12th Brigade. The Brigade rejoined the 4th Division from the 36th.	J.
MAILLY-MAILLET	6th		Dispositions of the Company as under:- Right Section Lt BOYD and Lt K.R.G. BROWNE with guns:- 1 gun in DELAUNAY Trench, 1 gun in HORSESHOE TRENCH, 2 guns in TAUPIN TRENCH (Divisional line). Left Section Lt LIGHTBODY and 2nd STRAIGHT with guns:- 1 gun in ROB ROY TR. 1 gun in NAIRNE ST. 1 gun in AITTITE TRENCH (Divisional line) 1 gun in PALESTINE TRENCH (Divisional line)	Ref PLEX TRENCH MAP 1/10,000 No 61. See Appendix "No 1" J.
do	7th 8th		Uneventful.	J.
do	9th		1 O.R. wounded. Remaining section detailed permanently to the Company by the Brigade.	J.
do	10th		Coy H.Q. moved to COLINCAMPS.	J.
COLINCAMPS	10th 11th		Lt BROWNE and 4 O.R. proceeded on a Vickers M.G. course to BERTRANCOURT. Transport lines to ST OMER. Positions of the forward guns in the left Sector were shifted as follows:- NAIRNE ST GUN to position in JORDAN TR. near TOUTVENT Tr. ROB ROY GUN to EXCEMA TR. These two guns on the enemy front line thus gave effective cross fire between these two guns on the enemy front line.	J.

WAR DIARY
or
INTELLIGENCE SUMMARY

(Erase heading not required.)

Army Form C. 2118.

Place	Date	Hour	Summary of Events and Information	Remarks and references to Appendices
COLINCAMPS	Feb 12–13th		Uneventful—	2
	14th		Complete relief in both Sectors. N.B. Tabards went numbers did not permit of complete change of company. Was 2 officers, completes from the 2nd Duke of Wellingtons Regt.	2
"	15th		Uneventful.	2
"	16th		All ran out of trenches fired a course on about range near billets	2
"	17th		Dugout for EXCEMA AVE. gunteam completed	2
"	18th		Complete relief in both Sectors	2
"	19th		Germans made a raid on the line held by the 2nd Lancashire Fus. (Right Sector) at 6.30 pm. Neither forward gun had an opportunity of opening fire. The enemy were driven back by reinforcements and Artillery fire. (By night, guns in the offensive positions in the support line, must have communication with the front line, if they are to know when to open fire. A supply of coloured Rockets or telephones would be invaluable)	2
"	20th		Experiments were carried out with Night Firing Stovepipe Flash Concealers. A pipe 6 ft long, was found to be far superior to the ordinary pattern on issue	2

Army Form C. 2118.

WAR DIARY
or
INTELLIGENCE SUMMARY.
(Erase heading not required.)

Instructions regarding War Diaries and Intelligence Summaries are contained in F. S. Regs., Part II. and the Staff Manual respectively. Title pages will be prepared in manuscript.

Place	Date	Hour	Summary of Events and Information	Remarks and references to Appendices
COLINCAMPS	Feb 21st		Arrangements were made with the 107th Company to give supporting fire at night on signal being given by lamp by Company of Infantry in the front line. Two fire to cover the ground in front of the QUAD RILATERAL Positions of Right Section guns approved by G.O.C. 12th Brigade	Ref. PLEX Trench Map No 61, 1/2
"	22nd			R.
"	23rd		Men of Company instructed in the use of the SALVUS Breathing Apparatus. Heavy fall of snow.	R.
"	24th		Relief of both Sections. Relief of these difficult as Company was still 2 Officers under strength.	R.
"	25th 26th		Uneventful.	R.
"	27th		4 N.C.O.'s returned from a course of Instruction in the use of the SALVUS apparatus. Also in the Care and inspection of Gas helmets and goggles. One of these men was allotted to each section for the purpose of supervising the above.	R.
"	28th		After a week of snow and an average temperature of 15° Fav. at night, the weather grew milder. The consequent thaw made a great deal of work necessary to keep the trenches in good condition	R.

Army Form C. 2118.

WAR DIARY
or
INTELLIGENCE SUMMARY.

(Erase heading not required.)

Place	Date	Hour	Summary of Events and Information	Remarks and references to Appendices
COLINCAMPS	Feb 29th		Relief in both sectors. Lt T.D SOUTHGATE and 2Lt K.F. BARRATT from 2nd Essex Regt. joined the company and completed the establishment of officers. The strength of the company was increased by the arrival of 16 men to being detailed from each battalion in the Brigade. All these men were trained in the use of the machine gun. They were sniped at but to the company as the relief could not be effectively carried out with the same teams. Establishment complete. Weather Snow : 12° frost at night	R. R.
"	March 1st		Uneventful - hard frost and snow.	R.
"	2nd		Officers of 144th Bde. M.G. Coy. here shown the trenches in both Sectors.	R. R.
"	3rd	5 pm.	Company was relieved in the line by the 144th Coy. Relief complete at 3.30pm. Company moved to SAILLY-AU-BOIS for the night.	R.
SAILLY-AU-BOIS	4th		Heavy Snowfall - Company moved to HALLOY, nights very cold - frost.	R.
HALLOY	5th		Move to BOUQUEMAISON. Roads very bad owing to melting snow.	R.
BOUQUEMAISON	6th		Uneventful.	R.
"	7th		Training programme to be carried out while the company was out of trenches was furnished to the 12th Brigade	R.

Army Form C. 2118.

WAR DIARY
or
~~INTELLIGENCE SUMMARY~~

(Erase heading not required.)

Instructions regarding War Diaries and Intelligence Summaries are contained in F.S. Regs., Part II. and the Staff Manual respectively. Title pages will be prepared in manuscript.

Place	Date	Hour	Summary of Events and Information	Remarks and references to Appendices
BOUQUEMAISON	March 8th		Uneventful.	
	9th			
BARLY	10-14th		Company moved to BARLY.	
	14th		Training.	
			In accordance with daily orders of the Machine Gun Corps (Infantry Branch) dated 14.3.16. The Company became No 12 Company, Machine Gun Corps and the personnel of the Company were transferred to the Machine Gun Corps and allotted numbers in the Corps in place of their old regimental numbers.	
	15th		2/Lt. R.G. BROWNE rejoined the Company from a machine gun course.	
	16th		Uneventful.	
	17th		Move to HALLOY.	
HALLOY	18th		Move to BAILLEULVAL. Officers reconnoitre gun positions in the line held by the 111th Company M.G. Corps.	
BAILLEULVAL	19th		Company relieved 111th Company in the line. Relief complete by 3 p.m. Disposition Right Sector Lt LIGHTBODY Left Sector Lt BOYD with 2 guns in FORT GASTINEAU 1 gun in the Ravine 2 guns ” ” 2 guns at Pt. 147. ALOUETTE 1 gun in FORT GASTINEAU 8 guns in Reserve in billets at BAILLEULVAL	See Appendix No 2. Ref PLEX Trench Map IV D1, Top Sect.

Army Form C. 2118.

WAR DIARY
or
INTELLIGENCE SUMMARY.
(Erase heading not required.)

Place	Date	Hour	Summary of Events and Information	Remarks and references to Appendices
BAILLEULVAL	March 20th		Uneventful.	R.
"	21st		111th Company left and company moved into billets vacated by them. 2/Lt STRAIGHT and SOUTHGATE returned from machine gun course at ST. OMER.	R.
"	22nd		Dugouts commenced in the RAVIN DES CUISINIERS for one complete section.	R.
"	23rd		Emplacements started in LINCOLN LANE and LLANDAFF LANE. New position chosen for the gun in trench 134 to enfilade enemy line opposite Centre of Left Sector. Site chosen also to protect ground in front of Right flank of 116th Brigade on the left of the 12th Brigade. Orders in the event of an alarm received from 12th Bde. On its receipt of orders to "move to position":— 2 guns move to TRENCH "A" 2 " " " CHINA WALL Remainder move to a position of readiness near RAVIN DES CUISINIERS.	R.
"	24th		Billets inspected by O.C. 12th Brigade. During night 23/24th there was a heavy fall of snow. This came very unexpectedly after a spell of warm weather, and caused a temporary cessation of work on the trenches.	R.

WAR DIARY

Army Form C. 2118.

Place	Date	Hour	Summary of Events and Information	Remarks and references to Appendices
BAILLEULVAL	March 25th		2Lt ROGERS returned from leave granted on Feby 27th but extended.	9.
"	26th		Relief in both sectors. Uneventful	12.
"	27th		Positions inspected by G.O.C. 12th Brigade. Up to this time the Company had always been short of two or more officers due to some being on courses of instruction in machine gun work. Sections were now permanently allotted as follows:— "A" Section Lt BOYD & 2Lt ROGERS : "B" Section Lt. LIGHTBODY "C" Section 2Lt BARR ATT & 2Lt BROWNE : "D" Section 2Lt STRAIGHT & 2Lt SOUTHGATE.	12.
"	28th.29th		Uneventful	12.
"	30th		G.O.C. 12th Bde. Inspected the 2 Sections of the Company resting in billets afterwards a tactical exercise was given by the G.O.C.	12.
"	31st April 1st–2nd		Relief in both Sectors. Uneventful	12. 12.
"	3rd		G.O.C. 3rd Army visited the line. Uneventful.	12. 12.
"	4th, 5th			12. 12.
"	6th		Guns in the support line allotted definite sectors of enemy line to harass regularly night and day	12.

WAR DIARY

INTELLIGENCE SUMMARY

Army Form C. 2118.

Place	Date April	Hour	Summary of Events and Information	Remarks and references to Appendices
BAILLEULVAL	7th & 8th		Uneventful	92
"	9th		2/Lt BARRATT and 10 OR proceeded on Vickers machine gun Course to ST. OMER.	92
"	10th		Uneventful	92
"	11th		FLAMMENWERFER demonstration	92
"	12th		Uneventful	92
"	13th	2 am	The 1st Bn. The King's Own Regt. carried out a successful raid on the enemy sap opposite trench 116. Two machine guns were fired on a known enemy machine gun to prevent the two gun firing across the enemy sap and stopping the raiding party. The raiding party were allowed 12 minutes to do their work and get clear of the sap and at the end of that time machine guns laid on the sap prevented the enemy attempting any reprisals. All arrangements worked successfully.	92
"	14th		No 18822 Sgt MARSH took over the duties of A/C.S.M. vice No 18778 Sgt HARTNEY (A)CSM since formation of company on Jany 24th 1916.)	92
"	15th		Divisional Gas officer inspected all anti-gas appliances in trenches	92
"	16th		Uneventful	92
"	17th		2/Lt R.F. BARRATT and 2/Lt K.R.G. BROWNE gazetted Lieutenants in the 3rd (S. Reserve Bn) The Essex Regt.	92

Army Form C. 2118.

WAR DIARY
or
INTELLIGENCE SUMMARY.
(Erase heading not required.)

Instructions regarding War Diaries and Intelligence Summaries are contained in F. S. Regs., Part II. and the Staff Manual respectively. Title pages will be prepared in manuscript.

Place	Date	Hour	Summary of Events and Information	Remarks and references to Appendices
BAILLEULVAL	April 18th		Relief in both Sectors.	92
"	19th		G.O.C. 12th Brigade inspected position in the line and suggested the provision of light shelters for guns in "harassing" positions. These were constructed with one sheet of corrugated iron and light uprights. Heavy dewy wet and caused great difficulty in carrying on very necessary work	92
"	20th 21st 22nd 23rd		uneventful	R.
"	24th		Relief in both Sectors.	R.
"	25th		Weather changed to bright sunshine and unusual heat.	R.
"	26th		uneventful	R.
"	27th		Lt BARRATT returned from M.G. Course.	R.
"	28th		uneventful	R.
"	29th		Officers of the 111th Machine Gun Company reconnoitred the line before taking over.	R.
"	30th		Company relieved by the 111th Company	R.
	May 1st	8.30 pm	Company marched off from BAILLEULVAL	R.
LE SOUICH	2nd	2.30 am	Company arrived at LE SOUICH	92

Army Form C. 2118.

WAR DIARY
or
INTELLIGENCE SUMMARY.
(Erase heading not required.)

Instructions regarding War Diaries and Intelligence Summaries are contained in F. S. Regs., Part II. and the Staff Manual respectively. Title pages will be prepared in manuscript.

Place	Date	Hour	Summary of Events and Information	Remarks and references to Appendices
LE SOUICH	May 3rd		uneventful	72.
"	4th		2nd S.W. HOOLE joined the company from M.G. Corps Training Centre at GRANTHAM thus completing the establishment to 10 officers	72.
"	5th to 6th		training	72.
"	7th		Move to BERTRANCOURT.	92.
BERTRANCOURT	8th		2nd R.S. GEDDES joined the Company from GRANTHAM.	92.
"	9th		training	92.
"	10th		Company inspected by the Commander in Chief of B.E.F	92.
"	11th		uneventful	92.
"	12th		Orders received from Brigade that company had to find a digging party of 100 men nightly, work was digging Cable trenches. All training Schemes had to be abandoned.	92.
"	13th 14th		Digging	92.
"	15th		A.D.V.S. inspected transport. Condition of horses and shoeing - good.	92.
"	16th – 22nd		Digging Cable trenches	72.
"	23rd	9.30 pm	Move to GORGES.	92.

Army Form C. 2118.

WAR DIARY
or
INTELLIGENCE SUMMARY.
(Erase heading not required.)

Instructions regarding War Diaries and Intelligence Summaries are contained in F.S. Regs., Part II. and the Staff Manual respectively. Title pages will be prepared in manuscript.

Place	Date	Hour	Summary of Events and Information	Remarks and references to Appendices
GORGES	24th	10am	Brigade was inspected on the march by Lt General Sir A. HUNTER-WESTON Commanding the VIII Corps to which the 4th Division had been transferred. Arrival at GORGES.	T.
"	25th	3.30am	Move to CUMONT FARM near YVRENCH	T.
CUMONT FARM	26th		The Brigade commenced to train for the coming attack. The company practised extension from column of fours into teams in file and thence into extended line, conforming exactly to the same movement by infantry. Particular attention was paid to the carrying of guns and tripods. Spare numbers carried belt boxes. Trenches were laid out on the ST. RIQUIER Training Ground corresponding to the enemy trenches in front of SERRE and toward the QUADRILATERAL and assembly trenches of the Brigade were arranged.	
"	27th		The Brigade practised the attack. "B" Section (4 guns) were told off to advance to enemy second line trenches with the 1st King's Own Regt. "C" Section (4 guns) and "D" Section (2 guns) to enemy front line with 2nd Essex Regt. and there to divide 2 guns to go with each of the 3Bns./ 1st King's Own, 2nd Essex and 2nd Duke of Wellingtons. (1 gun) A + D Sections in reserve with 2nd Lancs Fus.	It's See Appendix 3.

WAR DIARY or INTELLIGENCE SUMMARY

Army Form C. 2118

Place	Date	Hour	Summary of Events and Information	Remarks and references to Appendices
CUMONT FARM	May 27th		Carriers to assist the Machine Gun Company to carry belt boxes with ammunition were permanently detailed from Battalions in the Brigade. These carriers went to carry belt boxes in the actual attack and until the time of attack were both available for training with the Machine Gun Company in order that they might get to know the teams they were carrying for.	J.R.
	28th		Uneventful.	See Appendix 4.
	29th		Divisional Training Exercise.	Do.
	30th, 31st		Training practising the attack.	
	June 1st			
	2nd, 3rd			R.
	4th			
	5th, 6th, 7th		Brig. Gen. J.D. CROSBIE takes over command of the 12th Brigade from Brig. Gen. F.G. Anley training for attack.	R. R.
	8th, 9th		Brigade Sports. G.O.C. Brigade inspects Machine Gun Company	R. R.
GORGES BEAUVAL	10th		Brigade move to GORGES move to BEAUVAL	R.
	11th	4pm	Coy attend memorial service for the late FieldMarshal Lord Kitchener move to AUTHIE	R.
AUTHIE	12th		Uneventful.	
	13th		100 men under 2 officers were sent to billets at MAILLY-MAILLET to furnish digging parties for cable trenches	R.
	14th		Coy. H.Q. move to BERTRANCOURT with transport. Time advanced one hour at 11 pm so that 11 pm 14.6.16 became midnight.	
BERTRANCOURT	15th, 16th, 17th, 18th		Company digging at MAILLY-MAILLET.	R.

WAR DIARY or INTELLIGENCE SUMMARY

Army Form C. 2118

Place	Date June	Hour	Summary of Events and Information	Remarks and references to Appendices
BERTRANCOURT	19th		½ of company returned to BERTRANCOURT.	J.R.
"	20th		Remaining half of company returned to BERTRANCOURT from MAILLY-MAILLET.	See Appendix No 5
"	21st		Received copy of 12th Infantry Brigade Order No 18 dated 21 June 1916 containing orders for the attack which was to be made.	J.R.
"	22nd 23rd		Special training engaged in for the attack.	J.R.
"	24th		Preliminary Artillery bombardment of enemy's lines commenced.	J.R.
"	25th		Enemy began to shell billets in BERTRANCOURT.	J.R.
"	26th		training	J.R.
"	27th		Received copy of 12th Bde. Order No 19 dated 27/6/16 — Orders for the Assembly before the attack	J.R.
"				R.
"	28th		BERTRANCOURT again shelled. @ Q.M.S. J. TAYLOR and I.O.R. killed →	See Appendix No 5.
"			Received B.M. 4 (12th Bde) stating that "28th was to be "Y." Day → Received B.M. 6 of 28/6/16 to the effect that "Y" day was postponed and training had to be carried on as usual.	R.
"	29th		Received B.M. 9 of 29/6/16 to the effect that 30th was to be "Y2" Day and that the Assembly would therefore take place according to Bde. Order No 19 of 27/6/16	See Appendix No 5. J.R.
"	30th		Received B.M. 733 of 30/6/16 to the effect that the O.C. Brigade Signals would establish a telephone Station at Bde H.Q. in trenches at 8 pm on Y/Z night. is. on assembly night.	J.R.
"		5 pm.	Received B.M. 436 of 30/6/16 re Synchronising of watches. All watches synchronised at Brigade H.Q. 3 watches kept.	J.R.

Army Form C. 2118

WAR DIARY
or
INTELLIGENCE SUMMARY
(Erase heading not required.)

Instructions regarding War Diaries and Intelligence Summaries are contained in F. S. Regs., Part II. and the Staff Manual respectively. Title Pages will be prepared in manuscript.

Place	Date	Hour	Summary of Events and Information	Remarks and references to Appendices
BERTRANCOURT	June 30th		Received B.M. 10 of 30/6/16 to the effect that "Zero hour" would be 7.30 am on July 1st 1916 unless otherwise ordered	See Appendix No. 5.
"	"	5 pm	Company moved off to their places of assembly, preparatory to the Attack. Moving by BEAUSSART thence by Cross Country track to the SUCRERIE. Limbers were unloaded where the road from MAILLY-MAILLET to COLINCAMPS crossed the ACHEUX - MAILLY- MAILLET railway and thence guns and tripods with all gun equipment were carried by the teams and camera to the Assembly positions "B" Section moving to GREEN TRENCH (South end) with the 1st King's Own ½ C Section — to GREEN TRENCH (North End) with the 1st King's Own ½ C Section — 9+10 teams — to TAUPIN Support trench with the 2nd Essex ½ D Section — 13 +14 teams — to ELLES SQUARE with the 2nd Essex Coy H.Q. A Section ⎱ — to FORT HOYSTED. ½ D Section 15 +16 teams ⎰	
		11 pm	Assembly complete. reported to Bde H.Q. through Telephone Station at Bde H.Q. in trenches.	

WAR DIARY or INTELLIGENCE SUMMARY

Army Form C. 2118.

APPENDIX (1)

Place	Date	Hour	Summary of Events and Information	Remarks and references to Appendices
			12th Brigade DEFENCE SCHEME COLINCAMPS SECTOR.	Ref. 12th Bde 8M 541 of 9.2.16. Ref:- Trench Map HEBUTERNE 57 D N.E. 1/10,000 2nd Ed. Trench Map BEAUMONT 57 D S.E. 1/10,000 2nd Ed. Trench Map PLEX No 61. 1/10,000

The following details applied chiefly to the Company:-

Situation of Area. The front line, running due N. + S., extended from the SERRE - MAILLY-MAILLET road on the South to the SERRE - HEBUTERNE road on the North. The centre of the front line was 900 yds due W. of SERRE. The extent of frontage held 2500 yds.

Division of Area. Right Sector - trenches 78-86 inclusive
                 Left Sector -   87-95 inclusive

Boundary between Sectors - WARLEY ST to Junction of WARLEY + EXCEMA.

MACHINE GUNS. The Company to put (a) 2 guns in each Sector (b) 4 guns in 2nd Divisional line, i.e., 1 gun in PALESTINE, 1 gun in HITTITE, 2 guns in TAUPIN.

Reserve 8 guns in billets in COLINCAMPS.

Action on Signal "Move to Position". The Company to send
1 Gun to HITTITE TRENCH
1 gun to concrete emplacement N. of PALESTINE Avenue at K.21.d.2.1.
Remaining guns to go to a position of readiness near K.31.c

WAR DIARY
or
INTELLIGENCE SUMMARY.

(Erase heading not required.)

Army Form C. 2118.

APPENDIX N° 2

Place	Date	Hour	Summary of Events and Information	Remarks and references to Appendices
DEFENCE			12th Brigade. B.M. N°. of 22nd April 1916.	Ref. Trench Maps RANSART 51C S.E.3+4 parts of FONQUEVILLERS 57D NE 1 & 2 parts of PLEX IV Div. Topo Sect.

SCHEME

The following details applied directly to the Company:—

Line held by the 12th Brigade from point X.1.a.7.1. 800 yds S. of BELLACOURT to a point W.23.b.8.7. 1000 yds N. of MONCHY - AU - BOIS. The sector was divided into 2 Sub. Sectors. **Right Sub. Sector** trenches 113 - 127 (inclusive) Right boundary "FARN BORO'" Trench : Left boundary ROSCOMMON Road and FORT GASTINEAU.

Left Sub Sector Trenches 128 - 140 (inclusive) Right boundary : ROSCOMMON ROAD and FORT GASTINEAU. Left Boundary LLANDAFF LANE.

The permanent positions for the 8 guns in the line for the defence of the Brigade Sector were here :—

1 Gun in RAVINE pt W.17.d.4.1.
1 " " RENFREW ROAD W.17.b.4.4.
1 " " LINCOLN LANE W.12.a.9.4.
1 " " Point 147. (Fort)
2 guns in FORT GASTINEAU
2 " " FORT ALOUETTE
1 " " LIMERICK LANE X.1.c.2.7.

WAR DIARY
INTELLIGENCE SUMMARY.   APPENDIX No 2 Cont'd.

In case of attack by the enemy 4 guns from the Reserve Sections in billets in BAILLEULVAL move as follows.

1 .. to position in LLANDAFF LANE X.1.a.0.4.
1 .. .. .. LIMERICK LANE W.6.d.4.8.
1 .. .. .. FOLKESTONE Trench W.17.c.0.9.
1 .. .. .. FARNBORO " W.16.d.5.7½.

Remaining 4 guns move to the RAVIN DES CUISINIERS.

(a) Guns to be kept in their permanent positions in the line, unless being held for harassing operations. (b) Alternative positions to be constructed for each gun. (c) SALVOS Apparatus to be kept in position where the No 1 of the gunteam can quickly get at it. (d) Reserve S.A.A. to be kept at points where belt filling would take place. (e) All N.C.O's to know all emplacements in the Brigade Sector and the quickest way to them from different points in the line or from Reserve billets. (f) Emplacements to be numbered throughout the Sector from right to left. (g) Alternative positions to be numbered thus :— | M.G. 2.A | is alternative emplacement to No 2 emplacement

WAR DIARY or INTELLIGENCE SUMMARY

Army Form C. 2118

APPENDIX 3

(Erase heading not required.)

Place	Date	Hour	Summary of Events and Information	Remarks and references to Appendices
			12th BRIGADE ORDER	Ref. 12th Bde (Training) Order No 25 27/5/16
OBJECTIVES of 4th Division			The Division will take part in an assault on the German lines on the 27th inst. The 31st Division will be on the left and the 29th on the right. The objectives of the 4th Division are (1) enemy front line system of trenches from B19c 6.8 to A2 d 7.4. (II) enemy 2nd line system from B19c 2.5 to A18c 9.6. 3rd Objective — enemy 3rd line system from A35 a 6.8 to A22 c 37. (3) allotted to 10th and 12th Bdes.	
PHASES of the ATTACK.			(1) and (II) allotted to the 11th Inf. Bde. (3) Phases of the Attack. (1) Initial bombardment and wire cutting of 1st and 2nd objectives by Artillery. (2) 11th Bde attack, seize and consolidate 1st and 2nd Objectives (3) Artillery Bombardment 3rd Objective (4) 10th and 12th Bdes will attack and seize then consolidate the 3rd Objective. Boundaries between 10th and 11th Brigades will be marked by 2 large red flags. One at 2nd Objective, the other at 3rd Objective.	Ref. ST RIQUIER Training Map
ORDER of ASSEMBLY of 12th Bde			Units of the 12th Inf. Bde will assemble for the attack as follows:— 1st King's Own and 4 guns M.G. Coy in "LEGEND TR." 3rd Essex and 6 guns M.G. Coy in "ELLES SQ." 2nd Lanc. Fus and 12/1 T.M. Battery and 12/2 T.M. Battery at the SUCRERIE. Bde H.Q. and 6 guns M.G. Coy at FORT HOYSTED (B 8 b 3.1). Bde Signal Section B14 a 3.6. Advanced Dressing Station in dugouts near SUCRERIE at pt B 8 b 8.5. Reserve Ration and Water Dump at HYDE PARK CORNER pt B 14 A 3.5. Reserve Ammunition Dump and Reserve Bomb Dump at pt B14 a 3.5. On the Signal being given that the 11th Brigade have captured their objectives, the 12th Brigade will move forward to its 2nd Assembly Places as follows:— 1st King's Own from LEGEND to German 1st system in B19b 2nd Essex " LYCEUM " " " " B13c 2nd Lanc Fus t 12/2 T.M.B. " SUCRERIE & FT. HOYSTED " " " W. of SERRE Road 12/1 Duke of Wellington " ELLES SQ. " " " SE of SERRE Rd 4 Bde Machine Guns from LEGEND to enemy front line } 2 to King's Own new Assembly Place 6 Reserve Bde M. Guns from FT. HOYSTED to LEGEND } 2 " Essex 2 " Dukes	
ORDER of 2nd ASSEMBLY of 12th Brigade				

1875 Wt. W593/826 1,000,000 4/15 J.B.C. & A. A.D.S.S./Forms/C.2118.

WAR DIARY or INTELLIGENCE SUMMARY

Army Form C. 2118

APPENDIX (3) contd.

Place	Date	Hour	Summary of Events and Information	Remarks and references to Appendices
THE ATTACK ORDER of.			The attacks of the 12th Brigade will be carried out as follows:—	
			(a) Objective — Enemy trenches from ST. RIQUIER — YVRENCH Rd at Pt A35 a 7.7 to ST. RIQUIER — CAPENNES Rd at Pt A 28 b 8.4.	
			(b) Firing line and Supports 3 Battalions 6 Guns Bde M.G. Coy 12/1 T.M. Batty Special Mission 4 guns of Bde. M.G. Coy 12/2 T.M. By., 6 Guns Bde M.G. Coy Reserve 1 Battalion	
			(c) Advance — Firing line and Supports	Ref. ST. RIQUIER Training Map
		1	Left Battn — Kings Own — Objective from ST. RIQUIER – YVRENCHEUX Rd at A35a7.7 to A29 c1.9	
		2	Centre Battn — Essex — " " Pt A 39c 3.3 to A29 c1.9	
		3	Right Battn — Dukes — " " A 29 c 1.8. to A28 b.8.4.	
		4	Reserve Battn — Lan. Fus — to follow centre of advance about 300 yds behind the rearmost line advancing on a frontage of 400 yds and to take up position of readiness at Road between Pt A24 c 3.0 and A 24 c 2.9	
		5	Bde.Machine Guns — 4 guns from LEGEND take up position in enemy 2nd line near Pt 92 to cover advance of Brigade.	
			6 guns advance with units to 2nd line of Advance as under:—	
			2 with Kings Own on left flank	
			2 with Essex	
			2 with Dukes on right flank.	
			6 Reserve guns advance in rear of Lancs Fus and Yeoman in Reserve at X Roads at Pt A 30 a 3.8.	
		6	12/1 T.Mortar Battery will move with rearmost line of Dukes	
			12/2 T M By will move with rearmost line of Lancs Fus and Yeoman in Reserve at A24 c 2.8.	
		7	Bde H.Q. will move forward with the Reserve and on the right flank of the leading line of the Lancs Fus.	

WAR DIARY or INTELLIGENCE SUMMARY

Army Form C. 2118

APPENDIX 4

Place	Date	Hour	Summary of Events and Information	Remarks and references to Appendices
			12th Brigade Training Order (Amendment to Orders of 27/5/16) 28/5/16.	Ref ST. RIQUIER Training Map.

(1) The Division will take part in an assault on the German line on the 29th inst.

(2) The final objective of the Division is the enemy's third line of trenches from A33a6.8 to A22c3.7.

(3) The attack will be carried out as follows:—

1st Phase Intense bombardment and wirecutting.
2nd Phase 11th Bde. attack, seize and consolidate 1st and 2nd Objectives by Artillery. The Artillery will bombard 3rd Objective of 10th and 12th Brigades.
3rd Phase 10th and 12th Bdes attack, seize and consolidate their objectives. The 10th Brigade will be on the right and the 12th Bde on the left.

The Boundaries between 10th Bde and 12th Bde will be marked by 2 large Red flags one at 2nd Objective and the other at 3rd Objective as follows.

(4)(a) The units of 12th Bde will assemble for the attack as follows:—

1 King's Own + 6 guns M.G. Coy.   Assemble at LEGEND.
2nd Essex and 4   "   "   "   " LYCEUM
2nd Duke of Wellingtons and 12/1 T.M.By   " ELLES SQUARE
2nd Lancashire Fusiliers and 12/2 T.M.By   " SUCRERIE

Bde M.G. Coy. H.Q. y   " FORT HOYSTED.
and remaining 6 guns y
Bde H.Q. + Signal Section   " B14 a 3.6.
Advanced Dressing Station   " Dugouts near the Sucrerie B8 b 6.6.
Carryrie   " VALLADE (between HYDE PARK CORNER and BORDEN AVENUE)

(b) Reserve Ration and Water Dump   at HYDE PARK CORNER and B14 a 3.4
    Reserve Ammunition Dump   " VALLADE — B14 a 3.4
    Reserve Bomb Dump   " VALLADE — B14 a 3.
    Reserve Tool Dump   " Junction of VALLADE and SERRE Road.

WAR DIARY
INTELLIGENCE SUMMARY

APPENDIX (4) contd.

Army Form C. 2118

Place	Date	Hour	Summary of Events and Information	Remarks and references to Appendices

(5). 2nd Assembly Positions

1st King's Own from LEGEND to position of readiness in rear of Captured German 2nd line with leading line between Pt. B.19.c.4.7. and Pt. B.19.a.3.5.

2nd Essex from LYCEUM to position of readiness in rear of captured German 2nd line with leading line between Pt. B.19.a.3.5. and M.24.b.9.9.

2nd Ankers and 12/1 T.Mortar Batty. from ELLE'S Sq. to our front line on left of SERRE ROAD (T.M. By. moving in rear of Batt?)

2nd Lancs Fus and 12/2 T.M.By from SUCRERIE to our front line on right of SERRE ROAD (T.M.By. moving in rear of Battalion

A Bde Machine Guns from LEGEND to King's Own new Assembly place moving on left flank of 2nd line

B Bde Machine Guns from LYCEUM with Essex to their new Assembly place. 2 guns moving on Right of 2nd line

4 Bde Machine Guns from FORT HOYSTED to LEGEND to follow last line of DUKES

6 Reserve Machine Gun company 2 guns from A.35.a.7.8. to A.28.b.8.5 (Rect Flag).

12½ Bde will be carried out as follows:-

(6) The Attack

(a) Objective Enemy trenches from ST. RIQUIER-YVRENCHEUX Road at A.35.a.7.8. to A.29.c.3.5

(b) Disposition of Troops Firing line and Supports 2 Battalions. 12/2 T.M.By. 6 guns M.G.Coy and 12/1 T.M.By. 6 guns M.G.Coy.

Special Mission It guns M.G Coy Reserves 2 Battalions

(c) Advance to Attack from ST. RIQUIER-YVRENCHEUX Road at A.35.a.7.8. to A.29.c.3.5

Left Batt King's Own A.29.c.3.5 to A.28.b.8.5
Right Batt Essex will follow 800 yds in rear of King's Own
Left Res. B?n Dukes will follow 800 yds in rear of Essex
Right Res. Lancs Fus will not pass line A.25.c.4.5 See Para Y

Reserve Battalions from LEGEND take up position in Enemys 2nd line near pt. 92 to cover the Rifle Machine Guns (i) 4 guns advance with units as follows - A.30.a.3.3 with Kings Own on left flank, 2 with advance of Brigade (ii) 6 guns on Right flank 2 with Dukes on left flank, 2 with Essex on Right flank, 2 with Dukes and Remain in Reserve at X Roads pt A.30.a.3.8.

(iii) 6 Reserve guns advance in rear of Dukes

WAR DIARY or INTELLIGENCE SUMMARY

Army Form C. 2118

Appendix (A) contd

Place	Date	Hour	Summary of Events and Information	Remarks and references to Appendices
	12/1		TM. By will move with Rear most line of King's Own with Rear most line of Lancs Fus and remain in Reserve at A.24.c.2.8.	
	12/2		TM. By will move with Rear most line of Lancs Fus and remain in Reserve at A.24.c.2.8.	
Brigade H.Q.			will move forward when the Advance commences.	

(M) **Instructions for Attack.** The attacking Battalions will push home the attack with the utmost vigour. The Reserve who follows 800 yds in Rear of the attacking Battalions will not have to find A.23 or H.S. — A.30 a 2.3. Unless the attack is held up for want of reinforcements. Immediately the attacking battalion Capture their objective they will consolidate & against counter attacks from the front and flanks pushing out strong patrols to capture any guns and act as a covering force. Machine gun and Trench Mortar officers will immediately rally positions and mount guns. Bombing parties will be organised. If the attack is successful the Reserve will dig in on the line A.23 a H.5. — A.30 a 3.3. Reserve Ammunition will be sent forward from the Brigade dump to form a forward Reserve dump with the Reserve battalion near X Road A.30 a 3.8.

After the 2 leading battalions obtain the final objective the 2 leading Battalions will advance in extended order. Distances between 11th Bde companies in Reserve — 50 yds. Distances of support companies 100 yds. On arrival at action of leading Corps will build up firing line and dig in behind enemy parapet. The support objective will build up and dig in about 150 yds in rear of leading Corps. After leaving 11th Bde final Corps will continue to advance in Groups. Grenade carriers Objective the 2 Reserve Battalions will continue offensive operations (3 Sandbags per man, grenade carriers dyke for training operations Fighting Order as in offensive operations will not be carried)

(1) Dress for Tools 50 Rds S.A.A. and 24 grenades per man carried by 1 section from each company.

(2) Tools 20 picks and 24 shovels per company carried to wear distinguishing badges.
(3) Wire Cutters All on charge to be carried.
(4) Each Batt. will send 1 full S.A.A. Cart and Grenade wagon with grenades to report to Staff Capt in trenches at Bde H Qrs. at 2.30 pm.
(5) Carriers report to Staff Capt at Bde H.Q. in trenches at 2.30 pm. M.G. Coy carriers report to O.C. Coy at SUCRERIE.
(6) No men to drink from water bottle until final objective Captured and Consolidated.
(7) Lewis Guns 2500 Rds per gun will be taken into action. M.G. Coy 3500 rds per gun in action.
(8) Stokes Guns 100 yds per battery © Very Pistols 100 lights per Battalion 50 at Bn. H.Q.
(9) Casualties wounded on stretchers to be sent back to Advanced Dressing Station 6. Avenue and CHEERO TR. for evacuation. No other trenches to be used for this purpose. They will be marked by small red flags.
(1) Brigade Police Posts at junction of CHEERO and TAUPIN trenches; at junction of NEW GATE ST and TAUPIN. They will stop all stragglers moving to the rear and collect them
(2) Junction of ROMAN ROAD and TAUPIN, junction of 6th Avenue and CRESCENT Trench & Bde Dump, where they will be used to carry up a load to their battalion with small parties and send them to Bde Dump.

WAR DIARY or INTELLIGENCE SUMMARY.

Army Form C. 2118.

APPENDIX Nº 5.

Place	Date	Hour	Summary of Events and Information	Remarks and references to Appendices
			Orders and Dispositions for the Attack. Specially affecting Nº 12 Machine Gun Company. Taken from Operation Order Nº 1 of 12th Machine Gun Company dated	26/6/16. Ref. Maps 57.D NE 1/20,000 and 57.D. SE 1/10000 HEBUTERNE & BEAUMONT.
Para (1)			The VIIIth Corps will take part in an assault on the German lines on the — . This date will be known as "Z" DAY and the hour of the assault will be known as "ZERO HOUR". The 4th Division will attack in the Centre, the 31st Division on the left and the 29th Divs on the right. The 48th Divs will be in Corps Reserve.	
2.			The object of the attack is to seize the enemy trenches on the GRAND COURT - PUISIEUX Ridge from pont R 8 b.5.y. to pt L26 c 5.6. and to form a defensive flank from the latter point to our present front line at JOHN COPSE. The 12th Machine Gun Company will assist the assault of the 12th Infantry Brigade.	
3.			Objectives of the IVth Division. 1st Enemy system from the line pt 91 to pt 94 to pt 05. 2nd Enemy trenches from pt 53 — K36a 8.2 — K36a 8.2 — 3rd and Final Pt R. 26 3.0 — Pt 26 — Pt 90 — L26 C 7.6. The attack of the IVth Division on their final objective will be simultaneous with that of the 29th and 31st Divisions	
4.			The 12th Brigade Objective is from Point L32 d 2.6 (point 26) inclusive to L26 C 7.6.	
5.			Phases of the Attack.	
			The 11th Brigade will attack the German front line system and when this has been carried the 12th Brigade with the 10th Brigade on the right will advance to the Final Objective	

Army Form C. 2118.

APPENDIX No 5.

WAR DIARY
or
INTELLIGENCE SUMMARY.
(Erase heading not required.)

Place	Date	Hour	Summary of Events and Information	Remarks and references to Appendices

For the advance of the 31st Division see Appendix A at end.
1st Phase. 5 days Bombardment of the enemys trenches commencing on "U" DAY and a GAS attack.

2nd Phase. Intensive Bombardment with Artillery and Mortars. 3rd Phase 11th Brigade attack capture and consolidate the 1st and 2nd Objectives 4th Phase. Artillery bombard 3rd or Final Objective

5th Phase. 10th and 12th Brigades attack and seize the Final Objective and consolidate it

6. Disposition of the 12th Brigade in the attack will be:—
FRONT LINE BATTNS. 1st Kings Own on the left, 2nd Essex on the Right.
RESERVE BATTNS. 2nd Duke of Wellingtons on the Left, 2nd Lancashire Fusiliers on the Right.
The machine gun company will be disposed as follows:—
"B" Section – Special Mission: Teams 11 and 12 ("E" Sect) attached to 1st Kings Own under the O.C. that unit
Teams 9 + 10 ("C" Section) attached to 2nd Essex under the O.C. that unit: Teams 13 and 14 ("D" Section)
Attached to 2nd Essex under the O.C. that unit: Coy H.Q., "A" Section and teams 15 + 16 ("D" Section)
in rear of the 2nd Duke of Wellingtons (in Reserve)

7. Action of the Artillery. The Artillery will lift off the German front line at "ZERO HOUR", at which hour the Infantry will advance. There will be no Artillery fire N. of lines as under:—
(a) 1st Objective aft 0.20 (b) 2nd Objective aft. 0.45 (e) Wire on line Yiruning N, through Pioul 14
— P.45 aft. 2.30. (d) PUISIEUX Road line "C" aft. 2.40. (e) FINAL OBJECTIVE aft 3.30.
(f) Line 300 yds. E. of Observation line aft. 4.40. (g) Cease Fire 4.40.

Army Form C. 2118.

WAR DIARY
or
INTELLIGENCE SUMMARY.
(Erase heading not required.)

APPENDIX No 5.

Place	Date	Hour	Summary of Events and Information	Remarks and references to Appendices
			The Heavy Artillery will lift in all cases 5' mins before each of above lift. The Divisional Artillery at the commencement of each Infantry Attack will lift 100 yds and continue lifting at the rate of 100 yds in two minutes to the Objective firing 3 rounds of gunfire at each step.	
			The Heavy Artillery will lift straight on to the Final Objective. Infantry must not arrive at the successive objective before the times shown under above lifts, but must regulate their pace according to the above lift of Bom are checked by our barrage they will halt and wait until the barrage moves forward.	
	8.		The Company will Assemble for the Attack as under :—	
			B Section in GREEN TRENCH (South End)	
			11 & 12 teams (E Section) in GREEN TRENCH (North End) with 1st Kings Own	
			9 & 10 teams (C Section) in TAUPIN SUPPORT TRENCH with 2nd Essex	
			13 & 14 teams (D Section) in ELLES SQUARE (South front) with 2nd Essex	
			Coy HQrs A Section and 15 & 16 teams (D Section) in FORT HOYSTED.	
	9.		Instructions for the Attack. Time Table of Moves at end of this appendix	
			Action of Patrols. Strong Patrols (1 Officer and 5 groups of 6 N.C.O's and men) and 2 Lewis Guns from the 2 leading Battalions will advance according to Time Table and push through the 11th Bde advancing as the Artillery lift.	
			Action of Firing Line and Supports. The attacking battalions will advance in Artillery formation (column of Sections) each on a frontage of 400 yds having 8 platoons leading and 8 platoons in support the distance between lines of Sections	

WAR DIARY or INTELLIGENCE SUMMARY

Army Form C. 2118.

APPENDIX No. 5

Sections of the leading platoons will be :- 100 yds between 1st and 2nd lines, and 50 yds between the remaining lines. The distance between leading and supporting platoons will be 50 yds.

After passing the 11th Bde Final Objective they will open out to a frontage of 500 yds, remaining in column of sections, unless forced by fire to deploy. When the leading line of sections arrives on LINE "C" (PUISIEUX Road to PENDANT Trench), the whole Brigade will halt and strong patrols will push forward to get as close to the objective as our Barrage will allow. At 3.15 our advance will be resumed under cover of the Artillery and in the same formation (columns of sections) and will assault with the utmost vigour when within 40 yds of the Final Objective. On capturing the enemy's trench the leading battalions will push forward patrols to the line L32 a6.7 — L32b 6.5 — L26 c 9.6.

Which will be the Line of Observation and fighting patrols beyond that line to capture enemy guns. The remainder of the leading battalions will consolidate the captured position. They will make strong points as under: Strong Point A at Pt 33 (King's Own) B at P.90 (King's Own) C at Pt 12 (Essex), D at L32 a 1.9½ (Lancs Fus) E at L32 a 3.1 (Lancs Fus). These strong points will hold one platoon each. 2 Machine Guns and 2 Stokes Mortars and will eventually be joined up.

Action of the Machine Gun Company

Teams 11 and 12 will follow the 4th line of the 1st King's Own on the left flank.
Teams 9 and 10 will follow the 4th line of the 2nd Essex on the left flank.
Teams 13 and 14 will follow the 4th line of the 2nd Essex on the right flank.

WAR DIARY

Army Form C. 2118.

APPENDIX No 5 contd.

Place	Date	Hour	Summary of Events and Information	Remarks and references to Appendices
			They will imitate the formation of the battalions which they follow: on the advance they will help the attack of the Brigade by fire if required. On the capture of the Final Objective they will dig in in the Strong points as follows. Teams 11 and 12 in Strong Point A and Teams 9+10 in Strong Point B under O.C. King's Own. Teams 13+14 in Strong Pt C under O.C. Essex. They will mount guns ready to repel counter attacks. **Special Mission.** Officer i/c "B" Section will advance according to Time Table with the patrol of the 1st King's Own Regt. and will take up a position in the captured enemy position near Pt K 36 c 3.6. and cover the advance of the 12th Brigade to the Final Objective by bringing fire to bear on the Final Objective, and whenever possible, assist the advance of the 10th Brigade on the right. After 3.45 these guns will not fire on the Final Objective but will watch the left flank in case of counter attack and the officer i/c B Section will report his position by runner to O.C. Coy at Bn H.Q. near Point 63. Coy H.Q. "A" Section and Teams 15+16 will move in Artillery formation behind the last line of the 2nd Duke of Wellington's Regt to a position of readiness near Pt K36 a 7.5. If the assault on the final objective is successful the officer i/c "A" Section will take forward his section and mount guns (1) and (2) in Right Strong Point of the 2nd Duke of Wellington's S. of PENDANT COPSE. He will watch for counter attacks. Officer i/c Teams 15 +16 will remain in readiness near Pt K 36 a 8.2., and watch for counterattacks. **Communication.** During the advance Bn. H.Q. will move forward to the line MUNICH TRENCH, moving at K36 a 6.3. whilst reports will be sent a/to the advance. At 2.00. Brigade Forward Report Centre will be established from the 11th Bde Objective has started.	

10.

Army Form C. 2118.

APPENDIX No. 5.

WAR DIARY or INTELLIGENCE SUMMARY.

(Erase heading not required.)

Hour, Date, Place	Summary of Events and Information	Remarks and references to Appendices
	A Visual and Telephone Station will be established at or near L.31.a.3.3. The method of visual signalling will be repeated in succession. Messages to be repeated 20 V's in succession above messages will be used. Flares will be lit at the Final Objective when captured. Watches will be synchronised at 5.0 p.m. on Y Day. Succession of 5 Red Flares.	Report Centre will be established. Call up signal from front to rear. From front to rear with a narrow white stripe. They will wear a blue band with the indication of their position, by day or night is a S.O.S. Signal.
11.	Medical Arrangements. A Bearer subdivision will be attached to the Brigade and will move in rear of the 6th Avenue. Collecting posts will be established at the following points and will move in rear of the 6th Avenue. A Advanced Dressing Station at SUCRERIE D at Q.2.a.3.3. Casualties will be brought from Regimental Aid Posts to the most advanced of the collecting posts where they will be carried back by relays. Collecting Station will be established at Pt 45 when the Final Objective has been captured and Regimental Bearers will likely be advanced there.	Attack and will be established at the ROMAN ROAD at K.3 & 3½. 1.5½. Captured and Regimental Station will be established at Q.1.d.3.2.
12.	System of Supply. Normal System will be continued as long as possible. A Brigade Reserve of supplies and munitions will be established in the SUNKEN ROAD at L.31.a.3.1. 300 yds S.W. of PENDANT COPSE where S.A.A. Grenades will be taken by Brigade Carriers when the Final Objective is captured. Officer i/c Machine Guns will send a guide for their Reserve S.A.A. or water for the Guns.	A forward Reserve of PENDANT COPSE. 300 yds S.W. of PENDANT COPSE when the Final Objective is captured. S.A.A. or water for the Guns. ("M. ROGERS") will report to Brigade.
13.	TRANSPORT. Machine Gun Company Transport Officer will draw with Transport Officer at 6 pm "Y" DAY.	
14.	PRISONERS. will be dealt with by Battalion.	
15.	Equipment and Dress. (A) All Ranks of M.G. Company will wear Fighting Order. (B) Packs and Greatcoats will be stored in billets. (C) Each Man will carry also:- S.A.A., 1 IRON RATION, 1 Bandolier, 1 Cardigan, 2 Sandbags, 2 Smoke Helmets.	1 waterproof Sheet

WAR DIARY
or
INTELLIGENCE SUMMARY.

Army Form C. 2118.

APPENDIX No. 5
contd.

Place	Date	Hour	Summary of Events and Information	Remarks and references to Appendices
			Necessary Marching Equipment.	
			(d) Each Officer will carry one Very Pistol and 3 Very lights	
			(e) Each gunteam will carry 2 Shovels (carried on the Buck Under Equipment) A Section, B Section, Teams 9 +10, Teams 13 +14, Transport Officer 1 pair wirecutters each	
			(f) 5 pairs in all.	
	16.		Reinforcements. The T.D. SOUTH GATE and Pte GORING will report to Capt KOSTER DAA+QMG. 4th Div. on Y Day at J.33.c.9.4.	
	17.		Distinguishing Marks. All troops in the attack will carry triangular pieces of tin on their backs between the shoulders. The distinguishing mark for the 12th Machine Gun Company is Crossed Guns in the 12th Brigade Colour (RED) on the Sandbag Cover of their Steel Helmets.	
	18.		Maps and Papers. Only maps to be referred to or carried are 20000 Sheet 57 DNE. + SE and 10000 Maps 57 DNE + SE (HEBUTERNE and BEAUMONT) No maps showing our trenches will be carried on any other papers. Any maps or papers taken from the enemy are to be taken to Bde H.Q. Officers and N Cos will carry notebooks but no other papers	
	19.		Reports (a) Officer i/c M.Guns will render Situation Reports in writing not less than every ½ hour until final position is taken and then not less than 1 per hour, when more detail will be given. (b) Intelligence Reports will be sent to Bde H.Q. twice daily by team and 6 pm commencing 1 p.m. on "Z" Day.	

Army Form C. 2118.

APPENDIX No 5.

WAR DIARY
or
INTELLIGENCE SUMMARY.
(Erase heading not required.)

Place	Date	Hour	Summary of Events and Information	Remarks and references to Appendices
	20.		Casualties. Estimated Casualties will be reported to date to Bn HQ each hour commencing "ZERO" HOUR. Until final objective is captured, no man will fall out to assist wounded.	
	22.		Personnel for Attack.	
			Coy H.Q. O.C. Coy CAPT. G.B SLEIGH	
			A Section Lieut A.K. BOYD.	
			B Section Lieut K.R.G. BROWNE	
			C Section { 2 Lieut K.F. BARRATT.	
			{ 2 Lt S.W. HOOLE	
			D Section { 2 Lt R.M. STRAIGHT	
			{ 2 Lt R.S. GEDDES	
	23.		Reinforcements. 2 Lt E. ROGERS.	
			2 Lt T.D. SOUTHGATE	
			2 Lt J. LIGHTBODY	
	24.		Contact Air Patrol. During the attack 2 aeroplanes will be employed as Contact Patrols on the Corps Front. For sending messages to these and shutters will be issued to Bde H.Q. and all battalions. To denote the position of Bn HQ. and Bde HQ. a white groundsheet will be carried by each. To denote the position of the Scout Screen, flares will be lit should the line be held up, also immediately the final position is captured.	

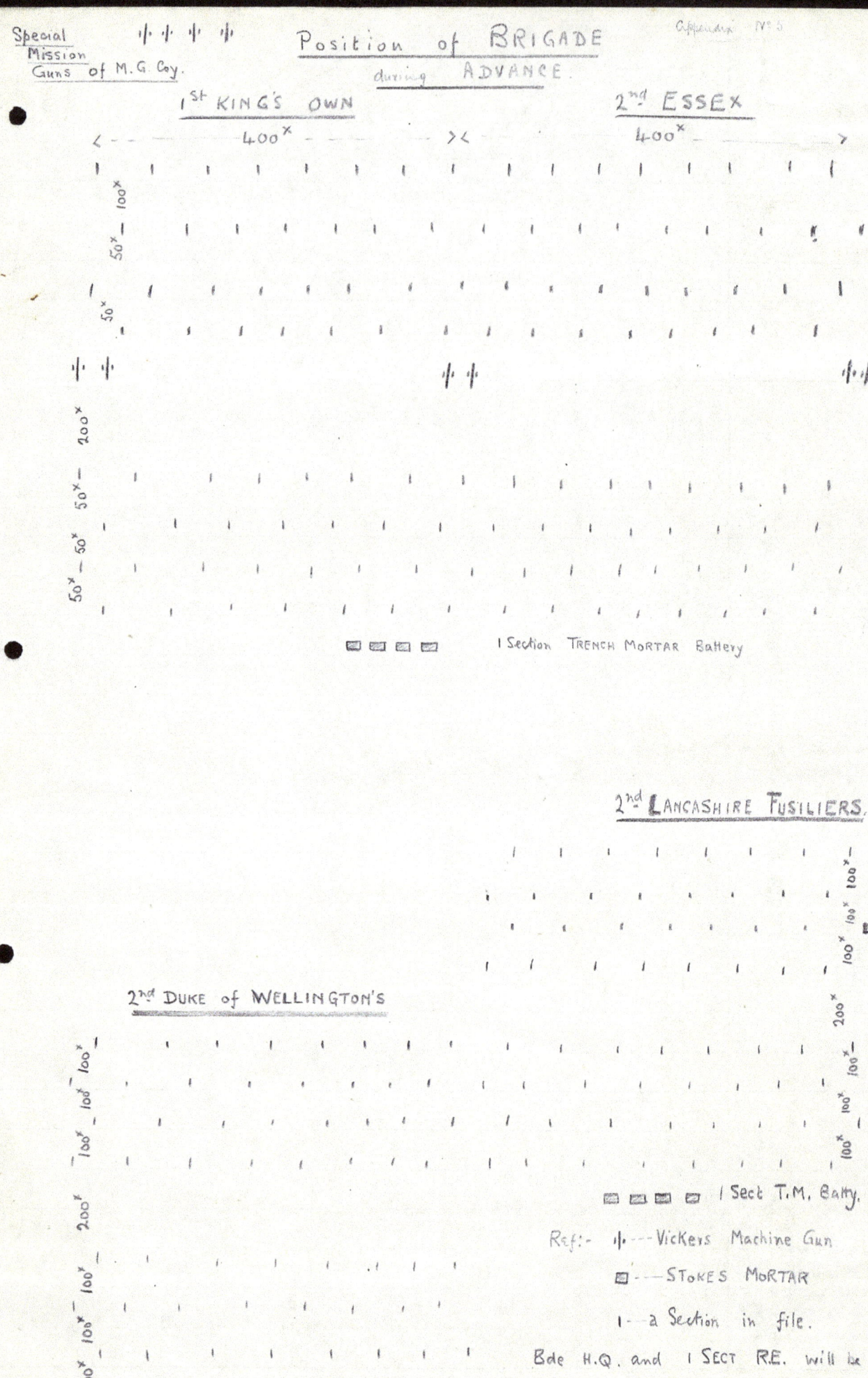

4th Division
War Diaries
12th Infantry Bde
M. G. Coy (FORMED 24-1-16)

January to August
1916

—

Jan 1918

CONFIDENTIAL

WAR DIARY

of

No 12 Machine Gun Company Machine Gun Corps.

From July 1st 1916   To July 31st 1916

Volume 1   appendices 6 & 7.

Army Form C. 2118

WAR DIARY or INTELLIGENCE SUMMARY

(Erase heading not required.)

Place	Date July	Hour	Summary of Events and Information	Remarks and references to Appendices
TRENCHES in front of SERRE	1st	7.10am 7.25am	Bombardment by guns of all calibres went on from 12 midnight to 7 am. Intense bombardment by Artillery and Trench Mortars commenced. 11th Brigade front line of attack got on parapet of their trenches ready to assault as soon as our Artillery lifted from the German front line.	
		7.30am ZERO HOUR.	Artillery lifted and 11th Brigade assault commenced. Enemy machine guns at once opened fire from the flanks. There was also a little rifle fire which increased as time went on. Even before 7.30 am while our artillery were bombarding very intensely an enemy machine gun began to traverse some of the parapets of the Assembly trenches. The enemy barrage was not put on at once when the 11th Brigade attacked. When but on it was in the centre of NO MAN'S LAND and all the Artillery of the enemy seemed to be participating in it so very few shells were seen to fall anywhere else. Owing to the amount of smoke and dust which overhung the area of conflict (the day being very hot with hardly any wind) it was almost impossible to tell whether the 11th Brigade attack had reached its objective but everything appeared to be going well. Enemy machine guns continued very active; about three guns were heard firing and were enfilading the attack of the 11th Brigade very effectively. Nothing could be seen of what was going on in the 31st Division on the left and in the 29th Division on the right	
		8.15 am	owing to the smoke and dust.	
		8.41 am	The 4 Special Missions Guns "B Section" left the Assembly trenches and advanced in Artillery formation in front of the 1st King's Own. At this time the enemy machine gun fire was very heavy and by the time NO MAN'S LAND was reached there were only sufficient men left to carry 1 gun into action and a useful supply of ammunition.	

Army Form C. 2118.

WAR DIARY
or
INTELLIGENCE SUMMARY.
(Erase heading not required.)

Place	Date July 13th	Hour	Summary of Events and Information	Remarks and references to Appendices
			This gun managed to get to the German front line but not without suffering more casualties to the gun team.	
		8.53am	2 guns of "C" Section advanced on the left flank of the 4th line of the 1st Kings Own. In this case also most of the teams were wiped out by machine gun and shell fire before they had got to the British front line, one gun and team being completely wiped out by a direct hit from a shell.	
		8.43 am	4 guns, 2 of "C" Section and 2 of "D" Section left the respective trenches of the 2nd Essex moving with the 4th line of that battalion. 2 teams of "C" Section on the left flank of the Essex and 2 teams of "D" Section on the right flank. The two teams of "C" Section suffered very heavy losses and one team was believed to have been blown up in a mine which the Refs. at R35a2.4 Germans exploded under our front line. The two teams of "D" Section on the Right flank got as far as the British front line without any casualties. By the time these two teams of "D" Section got to the German front line there were only about 4 men left and one gun having been hit and rendered useless by a bullet and the other had no tripod or ammunition left. as all the Carriers had been hit. Neither of these teams was able to come into action owing to the casualties they sustained	

WAR DIARY
or
INTELLIGENCE SUMMARY.

(Erase heading not required.)

Place	Date	Hour	Summary of Events and Information	Remarks and references to Appendices
	July 1st	9.10 am	The 6 Reserve guns and Coy H.Q. moved off in Artillery formation after the last line of the 2nd Duke of Wellingtons Regt "A" sector going in front. Nos 1, 2, 3 and 4 teams under Capt SLEIGH and Lt. BOYD followed by Nos 15 and 16 teams under Capt GEDDES. These teams got to our front line without many serious casualties, but white halted in No MAN'S LAND, owing to the advance of the infantry in front being delayed they suffered serious casualties through shell fire. Nos 1 + 2, and No 15 teams particularly, who lost almost all their carriers. Nos 3 and 4 teams got to the 2nd line of the German front line system and stood by there ready to mount.	
		11 am	That all was not going well in front became evident. The guns and fire of necessary. By this time it seemed an that all the flanks were being held up, as all the machine of the flanks were being held up, as all the machine gun fire was coming from the left flank where no advance seemed to have been made. On the right flank our forces seemed to have been held up also on the 29th Divisional front, and thus both flanks of the 4th division were in the air and quite unsupported. Owing to the heavy loss in Officers	

WAR DIARY or INTELLIGENCE SUMMARY.

(Erase heading not required.)

Army Form C. 2118.

Place	Date	Hour	Summary of Events and Information	Remarks and references to Appendices
	July 1/16	1 pm	of the units of the 4th division became very mixed up. The enemy began to make vigorous counterattacks with bombing parties up communication trenches and the enemy were now putting a heavy barrage all round those portions of their trenches which were occupied by the 4th division and so cutting off all communication either to flanks or rear. By this time it was seen that it was of no use trying to advance further, and a stand was made in the trenches around the QUADRILATERAL. The teams of the machine gun company helped by mounting all available guns but as the supply of belts and ammunition was too small, very little could be done. The teams which were left were also severely depleted.	
		5 pm	A message from Brigade H.Q. to the effect that guns of the Machine Gun Company were to reassemble in ELLES SQUARE reached two of the guns of company (D Section) which went back to the British front line stayed there for some time	

WAR DIARY
or
INTELLIGENCE SUMMARY.
(Erase heading not required.)

Army Form C. 2118.

Place	Date 1916	Hour	Summary of Events and Information	Remarks and references to Appendices
TRENCHES	July 1st		and eventually reached ELLES SQUARE having rather several boxes of ammunition on the way. The officer in charge 2/Lt GEDDES reported himself to Brigade H.Q. This message did not get to the guns in "QUADRILATERAL" until about 1.30 a.m. on July 2nd	
"	July 2nd	1.30am	Guns and teams in the QUADRILATERAL withdrew and reported to Brigade A.Q.	
		5 am	The day was spent in reorganisation of guntams Coy H.Q. was established in FORT HOYSTED. 9 guns were left of the 16 which had gone into action and their guns were posted in the Divisional positions and teams were kept as equal in strength as possible. An opportunity was also given of estimating the Casualties involved on the previous day.	
	Officers		Lt R.F. BARRATT Killed Lt A.K. BOYD, 2/Lt S.W. HOOLE and CAPT G.B. SLEIGH Wounded	
	Men		5 O.R. Killed 2 O.R. died of Wounds 51 O.R. Wounded 2 O.R. Missing	

WAR DIARY
~~INTELLIGENCE SUMMARY~~
(Erase heading not required.)

Army Form C. 2118.

Place	Date	Hour	Summary of Events and Information	Remarks and references to Appendices
TRENCHES	July 2nd		Of the 51 Carriers who had gone into action with the company to survived. The strength in trenches of the company on July 2nd was afterw 3 officers Lt R.G. BROWNE, Lt R.M. STRAIGHT and 2/Lt R.S. GEDDES and 62 O.R.	

WAR DIARY
or
INTELLIGENCE SUMMARY

Army Form C. 2118

Place	Date	Hour	Summary of Events and Information	Remarks and references to Appendices
TRENCHES at SUCRERIE MAILLY-MAILLET.	July 3rd		Received 14th Bde. Order No. 20 fixing Relief Table for week ending July 8/1916. M.G. Company to remain in their present position – Positions bombarded with tear shells. Battalion Commanders Conference held at Brigade H.Q. and precautions taken in view of a counter attack by the enemy. Unsuccessful.	P. A
do.	4th 5th		LIGHT BODY rejoined Company from 4th Army School. Coy H.Q. moved from FORT HOYSTED trenches to MAILLY-MAILLET. 2 guns here also withdrawn from the line leaving 7 guns in position. These were: (I) VALLADE TRENCH (N) (II) VALLADE TRENCH (near HYDE PARK CORNER) & Covering German Front line (III) TAUPIN TRENCH No 6 position { between QUADRILATERAL and REDAN (IV) TAUPIN TRENCH No 7 position { positions in Reserve in case their line broke (V) ELLES SQUARE (2 guns) enemy through our front line – (VI) FORT HOYSTED ——— Covering Right flank of Brigade Draft of 52 O.R. arrived at transport lines at BERTRAN COURT. Weather very wet and trenches very muddy.	P.
MAILLY-MAILLET and TRENCHES	6th	2.30pm	Draft arrived in MAILLY-MAILLET as Coy H.Q and were accommodated in Billets in cellars, as the town had been very heavily shelled with 5.9 inch shells.	

Army Form C. 2118

WAR DIARY
or
INTELLIGENCE SUMMARY
(Erase heading not required.)

Place	Date	Hour	Summary of Events and Information	Remarks and references to Appendices
MAILLY-MAILLET and TRENCHES	July 6th		2 Teams in the line relieved by teams formed of draft and spare men from Coy H.Q.	
	7th		Sgt. N. McMANUS rejoined Coy from 4th Army School. MAILLET-MAILLET very heavily shelled - which took place on the 30th June and 1st July. had to be rendered to Bde H.Q. in order to assist in compiling a Summary of events during the attack. 1 O.R. Wounded (Shrapnel)	T.I.
do.	8th 9th		Uneventful. 12th Bde Order No 22 of 9/7/16 received; orders for relief of 12th Brigade by 11th Brigade. 11th Coy Commander and officers reconnoitred the line. Capt. G.B. SLEIGH rejoined from Base after being wounded on July 1st and assumed command of the Company. Moved to Company relieved by 11th Machine Gun Company. Divisional Reserve at BERTRAN COURT.	
do.	10th	2pm	Relief complete.	
		5pm	Lt. W. E. ROBERTON 3rd Scottish Rifles att. Machine Gun Corps and Lt. C.L. KAY 11th North Staffordshire Regt and Machine Gun Corps joined the Company from Machine Gun Training Centre GRANTHAM.	

Army Form C. 2118.

WAR DIARY
or
INTELLIGENCE SUMMARY.
(Erase heading not required.)

Place	Date	Hour	Summary of Events and Information	Remarks and references to Appendices
BERTRAN- COURT	July 11th	2pm	Received B.M. No 600 containing new Code Names for units of 4th Division. These Code Names to be used in all telephone messages. Code Name for No 12 Machine Gun Company to be B.L.V. Company Muster parade held, and men of draft allocated to Sections. Reorganisation of Company. All Section officers visited the proposed machine gun positions on the "GREEN Line" of defence which had to be manned by the machine gun Company in divisional Reserve in case of attack by the enemy. These positions were:- (I) Q.1.d.2.4. — 1 gun (II) MILL at Q.1.d.8.8. — 3 guns (III) Q.1.d.5.0. — 1 gun (IV) Q.7.b.70.45. — 1 gun (V) Q.7.d.70.35. — 2 guns. 20 O.R. joined the Company from M.G. Corps Base Depot @ AMIERS Training and Reorganisation.	Ref:- TRENCH MAPS–FRANCE 57D.M.E. and S.E. parts of. Q.1 Q.2
do 12th do 13th do 14th			Training	

Army Form C. 2118.

WAR DIARY
or
INTELLIGENCE SUMMARY.
(Erase heading not required.)

Instructions regarding War Diaries and Intelligence Summaries are contained in F.S. Regs., Part II and the Staff Manual respectively. Title pages will be prepared in manuscript.

Place	Date	Hour	Summary of Events and Information	Remarks and references to Appendices
BERTRAN-COURT	July 15th		Received 12th Bde. Order No. 23 dated 15/7/16 re. relief of 10th Brigade in the line by 12th Brigade on 14th inst.	92
do	16th		Officers visit 10th M.G. Coy and reconnoitre the line held by No. 2/10 Machine Gun Company.	
do	17th	10 a.m.	Left billets in BERTRANCOURT and marched to MAILLY-MAILLET at Sq. P.14.b.	Ref: FRANCE TRENCH MAP 57D 1:20,000 M.E. & S.E. parts of.
Camp at P.14.b & TRENCHES	"	11.30 a.m.	"A" and "B" Sections leave for trenches: met by guides of 1/10 th M.G. Coy at AUCHONVILLERS level crossing. "C" & "D" Sect. & Coy. Hqrs. in reserve at P.17.D.	
		3 p.m.	Relief complete. "A" Section held the Right Sector (4 guns) and "B" Section the Left Sector (4 guns). Gun positions were:—	
			Right Sect: (I) PILK ST. } Covering enemy front (II) CRIPPS CUT. } line & No Mans Land (III) AUCHONVILLERS CEMETERY } Defence (IV) " " LEFT } of guns (Reserve)	
			Left Sect: (I) 4th Avenue } front line defence (II) KING ST. } guns (III) BOWERY (I) } Support (IV) BOWERY (II) } guns	
	"	10 p.m.	Received B.M. No. 459 ref. operations by 4th Division to assist 4th Army. These operations did not take place, the wind being unfavourable for the discharge of gas. No Raid took place. The machine guns however fired according to programme.	Ref: 4th Army Appendix No. 7:- 92

2353 Wt. W2544/1434 700,000 5/15 D. D. & L. A.D.S.S./Forms/C. 2118

Army Form C. 2118.

WAR DIARY
or
INTELLIGENCE SUMMARY.
(Erase heading not required.)

Instructions regarding War Diaries and Intelligence Summaries are contained in F.S. Regs., Part II. and the Staff Manual respectively. Title pages will be prepared in manuscript.

Place	Date	Hour	Summary of Events and Information	Remarks and references to Appendices
Camp at P17 band TRENCHES	July 18th	5 a.m.	Commenced Harrassing operations as per attested number of guns. Enemy firing positions were closer and sandbag firing platforms erected.	See Appendix No 6.
		8 p.m.	Enemy firing ceased. Owing to the fact that the Brigade was going to dig a new front line from BRIDGE END to join SUNKEN ROAD at Q.4.d.4.5.9½ and complete work on line begun by 13th Bde from North end of SUNKEN ROAD Q.4.d.5.7 to join No 9 Sap. I.O.R. joined Company from M.G. Corps Base Depot CAMIERS	Ref France 57 D 1:10000 Ref 12th Bde Digg up Sap BM 475.
do	19th	5 a.m.	Harrassing operations continued as on 18th	
		8 p.m.	Harrassing ceased as work was going to continue on new front line.	A
do	20th		Received 12th Bde Order No 24 dated 20/7/16 re relief of Company on 21st inst by 35th M.G. Coy—	A
do	21st	10 a.m.	I.O.R. wounded (Shrapnel) Relieving unit arrived in trenches, Section officers were shown dispositions.	A
		2 p.m.	Relief complete — Relieved Sections march back to Camp at Coy HQ.	
		3.30 p.m.	Company march off by BERTRANCOURT and LOUVENCOURT to	
VAUCHELLES -LES- AUTHIE		4 p.m.	VAUCHELLES - LES - AUTHIE — arrive in Camp there. Limbers were hooked ready to move off next morning.	F

2353 Wt. W2344/1454 700,000 5/15 D. D. & L. A.D.S.S./Forms/C. 2118.

WAR DIARY or INTELLIGENCE SUMMARY.

Army Form C. 2118.

Place	Date	Hour	Summary of Events and Information	Remarks and references to Appendices
VAUCHELLES-LES-AUTHIE	July 22nd	7am – 10am	Move off to AUTHIEULE. Arrive at AUTHIEULE and go into billets for the day. Received entraining orders. A Section of the Company with transport was to be attached to each Battalion in the Brigade for entraining purposes. Section officers reported to the Battalion Commanders under whose command they were to be during the journey and received instructions as to time of moving off for entraining. B Section to go with 1st King's Own Regt which left DOULLENS at 11.19 a.m. 23rd. C — 2nd Lancs Fus — 3.19 — D & Coy H.Q. — 2nd Essex Regt — 5.19 — A — 2nd Duke of Wellington's — 7.19 — Transport was in Lorry Cars sent on two hours before time of leaving DOULLENS STATION to allow of its being entrained in good time before the train left.	do.
	23rd	7am	B Section arrived at CASSEL Railway Station, the others arriving at about 2 hour intervals — Billets allotted to Company near HOUTKERQUE — and arranged billets	
		2.30pm	B Sect. arrived at D 18 b 3.7 near HOUTKERQUE — and arranged billets farm at D 18 b 3.7 before the arrival of Company.	

Army Form C. 2118.

WAR DIARY
or
INTELLIGENCE SUMMARY.
(Erase heading not required.)

Instructions regarding War Diaries and Intelligence Summaries are contained in F. S. Regs., Part II. and the Staff Manual respectively. Title pages will be prepared in manuscript.

Place	Date	Hour	Summary of Events and Information	Remarks and references to Appendices
FARM at D18b3.7	July 23rd	9pm	Last Section of Company arrived — Arrival of whole of Company reported to 12th Brigade Hqa. at HOUTKERQUE. Company training. 4th Division now attached to XIV Corps and now permanently in the 2nd ARMY Area.	Ref BELGIUM & FRANCE 2nd NE & NE 2 1/EMS 1/20,000.
do	24th			

Army Form C. 2118

WAR DIARY
or
INTELLIGENCE SUMMARY
(Erase heading not required.)

Place	Date 1916	Hour	Summary of Events and Information	Remarks and references to Appendices
Farm at D18 637 near HOUTKERQUE	July 25th		Company training in machine gun work. Capt. G.B. SLEIGH 1st Kings Own Regt. O.C. Company left to join the Staff of the A.P.M. 4th Division. Lt. W.R.G. BROWNE 3rd Essex Regt. assumed command of "B" Section the company. "Lt. C.L. KAY assumed command of "B" Section the company.	Ref: BELGIUM + FRANCE 27 N.E. 2 MEd 1:20,000
"	July 26th		Company training. Received orders to move up to the line the 12th Brigade to be in divisional reserve and to relieve the 3rd Guards Brigade Machine Gun Company. 2Lt. W.L. FRICKER 3rd York and Lancaster Regt. att. M.G. Corps joined the Company from GRANTHAM, England via CAMIER and was posted to "C" Section as Sub Section officer.	Ref Map.
"	July 27th 9am		Officers of the 1st Guards Bde. Machine Gun Company arrived at Company Billets and took over the billets. Lt. ROBERTON proceeded in advance of the Company to take over new billets at A 22.d 7.3. Stores were sent on by motor lorry.	Ref Trench Maps BELGIUM 28 N.W. Edition 3D
"	"	1.50 p.m.	Company marched off moving by WATOU, ST. JAN ter BIEZEN and POPERINGHE to camp at A 22.a 7.3	Ref. do
"	"	6.15 p.m.	Company arrived at camp. Arrival reported to General Brigade. H.Q. at A 30.d. Lt. BROWNE and 2Lt. LIGHTBODY reconnoitred machine gun positions in the "E" line of defence running through ELVERDINGHE, WOOD at B 23.a, BRIELEN and CHATEAU TROIS TOURS. for use in case this line had to be manned in case of attack from the N. The quickest and best routes also reconnoitred Camp at A 22.d	Ref do Ref. do

WAR DIARY or INTELLIGENCE SUMMARY

Army Form C. 2118

Place	Date	Hour	Summary of Events and Information	Remarks and references to Appendices
Camp at A22 d 7.3.	1916 July 28th		Section officers Lt GEDDES, Lt KAY, Lt ROBERTON, Lt FRICKER and Lt STRAIGHT with Section sergeants reconnoitred the "L" line of defence during the day.	Jr.
Camp at A22 d 7.3.	July 29		Lt K.R.G. BROWNE and Lt LIGHTBODY went up to the 10th Machine Gun Company Headquarters on the Canal Bank and also to reconnoitre the Right Section Machine Gun defences. Found that it was not possible to visit many of the gun positions by day owing to the absence of communication trenches. One of the 16 guns of the Company were in position and the other half Company was manning them with half teams for relief purposes. Coy HQ was on teams in reserve at Coy HQ near the YPERLEE about C 25 a 5.4.½.	Ref Trench Map BELGIUM 28NW Edn 3D Jr.
"	July 31st		Received orders from 134 Brigade to relieve Lt Gunn of the 11th Machine Gun Company 2 in ELVERDINGHE and 2 in WOOD at B Lt GEDDES was sent up to reconnoitre the position and found only 2 guns in the Wood at B 23 b and now in ELVERDINGHE itself.	Ref do-
		9.30pm	Relief party consisting of Lt GEDDES, Lt Bynoe and the whole of "A" Section (2 OR.) moved off to relieve 11th Brigade and B 23 b and ELVERDINGHE. Lt GEDDES Headquarters with grenade of 12th Brigade Headquarters in ELVERDINGHE. Completion of relief was reported to 11th Machine Gun Chateau. Lt K.R.G. Browne visited the Headquarters of the Company during the day to arrange for the above relief. Arrangements were made for Staffs of Rations and water to be sent in nightly to this Section.	Jr.

31/-

WAR DIARY or INTELLIGENCE SUMMARY

Army Form C. 2118

APPENDIX N° 6

Machine Gun Operations Ex BM 470 of 19/7/16

(1) Object of operations To harass enemy's likely withdrawal.
(2) The following places will be fired on continuously during the day commencing 5 am 18/7/16

Indirect and direct fire will be employed. Short bursts every five minutes on more o/ca.

TARGETS. (a) WAGON ROAD from Q5c.9.2. to Q5 d 4.8½. Special attention being paid to entrance to communication trenches (1 GUN)

(b) Entrance to communication Trenches on EAST and WEST of WAGON ROAD (1 GUN) at Pt 14.32

(c) STATION ROAD from Q11 a 7.7. to entrance to communication trench (direction) MINDEN TRENCH (2 Guns)

(d) Sweep BEAUMONT – HAMEL with frontal fire (2 GUNS firing from Q5d 8½.1. to Q12 a 9½.8½ (1 GUN)

(e) Communication Trench from Q5d 8½.1. to the road west Quarry CEMETERY

(f) "Y" RAVINE Special attention to QUARRY East of it to be paid. 1 GUN to carry out the firing

Extra guns to be sent up from the Brigade Reserve to Reserve.
and least 4 guns to be kept in Reserve.

Army Form C. 2118

APPENDIX N° 4.

WAR DIARY
or
INTELLIGENCE SUMMARY
(Erase heading not required.)

Place	Date	Hour	Summary of Events and Information	Remarks and references to Appendices

Extracts from 12th Bde H.Q. B.M. of 17.7.16.

(1) To receive information of 1st Army, the 10th Brigade will carry out operations below mentioned on night of 17/18th. The 10th Brigade carrying out a raid.

(2) Programme timed from ZERO hour which will be notified to O.C. 2nd D/Wellingtons Regt. and O/C. Gas discharge arrangements. This officer will be stationed at the junction of BROADWAY and ESSEX ST. and will be in telephone communication with O.C. Dukes.

(3) Code Words for Gas discharge.
   i. Wind favourable for discharge of gas .... "BERLIN"
   ii. " not " " " .... HANOVER
   iii. Is wind favourable for discharge of gas? .... COLOGNE ...... FRANKFORT

(4) To drown the noise of discharge of Gas from 8.10 to O.C. 12th Bde. M.G. Coy will fire during discharge :—
   12. (a) from ZERO HOUR to 1.10 (10 minutes)
       (b) from 1.10 to 1.30   (20 minutes)

The latter to commence 1 hour and 10 minutes after ZERO Hour.

Target BEAUMONT HAMEL approaches to it. No guns to fire S. of the Yunning through Q10 central — Q11 central Lying will not be fired from Battle positions Occasional short bursts of fire will be fired into BEAUMONT HAMEL and approaches to it from 10.0 p.m. onwards.

(5) O.C. Battalion will then the line and get all Routes in good dugouts by ZERO hour. Bombing parties will be kept ready, in dugouts to move out of Trenches.

WAR DIARY
or
INTELLIGENCE SUMMARY

Army Form C. 2118

APPENDIX N° 4

Place	Date	Hour	Summary of Events and Information	Remarks and references to Appendices
(6)			No reference to Operations except by code will be sent on any telephone.	
(7)			Watches will be synchronised from Brigade Signal Office at 8.0 p.m.	
			PROGRAMME of ATTACK	
			Frontage. Q.10 d.31 – Q.10 b 26	
		From To	Nature of Attack	Remarks.
		0.0 0.10	Gas discharge	Noise to be drowned by M.G. fire
		0.15 0.20	Bombardment 18 pr Shrapnel	Front and communication trenches
		0.30 0.35	do do	"
		1.10 1.30	Discharge of remainder of Gas	All cylinders to be closed at 1.30.
		1.40	Raid by 29th Division and 10th Brigade	10th Brigade on Craters on enemy trenches opposite ROONEY'S SAP.
		1.45 2.0	Artillery Bombardment (Steady Barrage)	

12th Brigade
4th Division.

12th INFANTRY BRIGADE

MACHINE GUN COMPANY

AUGUST 1916

Army Form C. 2118.

WAR DIARY
or
INTELLIGENCE SUMMARY.
(Erase heading not required.)

Instructions regarding War Diaries and Intelligence Summaries are contained in F. S. Regs., Part II. and the Staff Manual respectively. Title pages will be prepared in manuscript.

Place	Date	Hour	Summary of Events and Information	Remarks and references to Appendices
Camp at A.22.d 7.3.	1916 Aug 1st		Uneventful	Ref. BELGIUM 1/Sheet 28 N.W. 1:20 000
	2nd		Received orders to relieve 10th Machine Gun company in the line on the night of the 3rd/4th inst	
	3rd		Sent two guns to Ordnance 4th Division for overhaul	
		8.15 pm	Company moved off to relieve the 10th company. Lt GEDDES of "A" Section received orders to collect his four guns together and join the company outside BRIELEN at pt B28 b 9.5. For this purpose 2 limbers were sent off to ELVERDINGHE at 8 pm and to wood at B.23.a. Rest of company was by xxxxx track to the wood in A.30 thence by cross country track leading direct to CHATEAU TROIS TOURS, through BRIELEN and thence to CANAL BANK at C.25.a.2.8.	
		16.15 pm	Lt GEDDES with A Section arrived at B.28 b.9.5. where company had halted to await his arrival	
		10.45 pm	Company arrived at CANAL BANK. Guides of No 10 M.G. Company were in waiting there.	

Army Form C. 2118

WAR DIARY or INTELLIGENCE SUMMARY
(Erase heading not required.)

Place	Date	Hour	Summary of Events and Information	Remarks and references to Appendices
YSER CANAL BANK at C25a 5.5 (YPERLEE)	Aug 4th		LT. ROBERTON 2Lts FRICKER and KAY and 2Lt STRAIGHT had gone up to 10th Company HQrs to take over trench stores and see the gun positions before the relief took place. Relief was completed about 3 am. Disposition of the 10th Company in the line was as follows:- The line taken over from the 10th Company was divided into 3 Sector. (1) The left Sector comprised a group of four guns of two forward positions at CLIFFORD'S TOWER pt C21a 30.75 and KNARESBORO' CASTLE C.14d 8.1 and two rear guns in the reserve system of defence to be used as stopping positions in case the enemy broke through our front line at FOCH FARM C20 b 1.0. and LONE WILLOW C20 b 65.15. Officer in charge of this sector was 2Lt STRAIGHT with his headquarters at left battalion HQrs C20 d 4.4. (II) The Centre Sector comprised 3 guns at X9 in the "X" line of defence pt C27 a 75.50, THREADNEEDLE ST C27 b 3.5, and CROSS ROAD FARM C22 c 3.8. The first two guns were in the reserve line and the third gun was in the front line and was the only gun in the Coy. Sector that could fire an ordinary times (III) The Right Sector comprised 3 guns the first in the front line at B1b emplacement pt C 21 a.9.7. the second in HILL TOP FARM C21 d 2.9, the third in VIEW FARM C21 C 9.6. The two last mentioned guns were "stopping" positions. The guns to the Brigade Sector were HILL TOP FARM which stood on fairly high ground and FOCH FARM which was also a very Commanding position. Both places were strongly defended and contained stocks of- rations and	Ref. Trench Map BELGIUM 28 NW. 3 Edition 1:20,000.

WAR DIARY or INTELLIGENCE SUMMARY

Army Form C.2118

Place	Date	Hour	Summary of Events and Information	Remarks and references to Appendices
YSER CANAL BANK at C.25.a.5.5 (YPERLEE)			and water, S.A.A. etc. (iv) The Reserve positions were at WILSON FARM E. and WILSON FARM N Pt C.26.b.30.15 and CANAL BANK E.C.25.d.6.3. (v) The remaining 3 guns were held in reserve at Company H.Q. but one has guns were in Ordnance for Overhaul and only one gun was in reserve. And was intended for Anti-aircraft work. It was not possible to send in complete teams with the guns in the line as the Company was in trenches for a period of 16 days so 3 men per team of the 13 teams in position were sent up with their guns and the remaining 3 men of each team were retained at Coy H.Q. for relieving purposes. In all with the 3 complete reserve teams at Coy H.Q. there were 40 men in reserve at Coy H.Q. The relief of the teams in position was to take place every four days. Lt ROBERTON and Lt TRICKER were in charge of the right and centre sector respectively with their HQs at C.27.b.3.5. It was not possible to visit many of the gun positions by day. Owing to the absence of Communication trenches and the vigilance of the enemy. The question of control was therefore quite out of the sector officers hands. If an attack by the enemy took place. And Control was entirely vested in the team Commanders hands. To establish a liaison between the machine gun company and the Battalions holding the line, Officers i/c of machine gun sectors were to report nightly to C.O's of Battalions in the front line and teams had also to find out the position of the nearest infantry company H.Qrs. So that fire might be opened	

WAR DIARY or INTELLIGENCE SUMMARY

Army Form C. 2118

Place	Date	Hour	Summary of Events and Information	Remarks and references to Appendices
YSER CANAL BANK at C.25.a.5.5 (YPERLEE)			Quickly and effectively. Distribution of Reserve Ammunition on taking over the trench was as follows:—	
			FOCH FARM 39 filled Machine Gun Belts + 9000 Rds S.A.A. / CROSS ROAD Fm 24 filled belts + 2000 rds S.A.A.	
			LONE WILLOW 25 " " " 5000 " / THREADNEEDLE ST 30 " " " 5000 "	
			KNARESBORO' CASTLE 24 " " " 8,000 " / XQ 30 " " " 3,000 "	
			CLIFFORD TOWER 34 " " " 8,000 " / WILSON Fm E. 30 " " " 4,000 "	
			B 16 30 " " " 2,000 " / WILSON Fm N. 30 " " " 2,000 "	
			HILLTOP FARM 30 " " " 3,000 " / CANAL BANK E. 24 " " " 11,000 "	
			VIEW FARM 30 " " " 3,000 " / Coy H.Qrs. 30 " " " 26,000 "	
			In all 102,500 rds in filled belts and 91,000 rds of S.A.A. in bandoliers	
	Aug 5		Received a copy of 12th Brigade Provisional Defence Scheme for the Brigade Sector.	
		8.30am	Received signal "GAS ALERT" from Brigade HQ meaning that the wind was favourable for the use of gas by the enemy and that all men had to be on the alert with gas helmets ready for instant use. Water supply on the company front, out was being used by the division while the company was in the line. A system of supply of water had to be arranged. 28 petrol tins holding 56 galls of water to be brought up nightly with the Ration limbers for drinking purposes while 28 empty tins were sent down each night to come up filled on the following night.	
	Aug 6		The 87th Machine Gun company relieved the 112th Company. Positions gun visited and then reference to those on the immediate right flank of No. 12 Company, in C.25 the right flank of	it.

Army Form C. 2118

WAR DIARY or INTELLIGENCE SUMMARY

(Erase heading not required.)

Place	Date 1916	Hour	Summary of Events and Information	Remarks and references to Appendices
YSER CANAL BANK C.25.a.5.5 (YPERLEE)	Aug 6th		The 12th or the left flank of the 87th Bde was at any time exposed to a hostile attack. Weather still fine but not so hot. There has been about a fortnight of continuous fine weather, very hot during the day. The general direction of the wind has been from N. to N.E. but very variable. The line on Aug 4th has been from N. to N.E.	Fr.
	Aug 7th Aug		In Strength in both Sectors by ½ teams from Coy H.Q. The following is an extract from Routine Orders by Brig. Gen. J.D. CROSBIE Commanding the 12th Infantry Brigade (Aug 7th 1916):— "With reference to the recommendations for immediate reward for action on July 1st 1916 The Corps Commander has under authority granted him by His Majesty the King, awarded the "Military Medal" to the NCO's and men mentioned below. 12th Machine Gun Company.	
			18820 Sgt a.C.S.M S. WARD 18879 Sgt J. BERTENSHAW 18745 Cpl G.R. ALDHURST 18775 Pte A. WATSON These medals were presented to the about NCO's by General Sir HERBERT C.O. PLUMER G.C.M.G, K.C.B, Commanding the Second Army on the 7th August 1916. N° 18879 Sgt J. BERTENSHAW was not present being in hospital in ENGLAND wounded. 2/Sgt GLENN proceeded to join a course at 2/Lt R.M STRAIGHT and the 4th Divisional School of Instruction. Commencing 8th August 1916.	Fr.

WAR DIARY or INTELLIGENCE SUMMARY

Army Form C. 2118

Place	Date	Hour	Summary of Events and Information	Remarks and references to Appendices
CANAL BANK Aug 9th at C.25.a.5.5. (YPERLEE)	1916	10.15 pm	3 O.R. left Coy H.Qrs en route to the Machine Gun Corps Base Depot at ETAPLES. Orders to send them away had been received in the Company. Was 3 men over war establishment. Enemy opened a very heavy bombardment on the front held by the 12th Infantry Brigade. Particular attention was paid to the Suffolk lines and positions in and around farms. Heavy guns of all calibres up to 8.2 in here employed, as well as very heavy minenwerfer, which were fired in salvoes of six. During the bombardment the enemy searched the whole front and points behind the line shoot accurate machine gun fire. All our gun teams were immediately to arms. Immediately the bombardment commenced. Shells and minenwerfer fell very close to the gun positions and a direct hit was reported on the machine gun emplacement at CROSS ROAD'S FARM. The gun was put out of action through the emplacement falling on it. Another gun from the reserve guns at Coy Hqs was sent up to replace it as soon as possible. The ammunition for this gun was also buried by the shell explosion and had to be extricated. There was one casualty. No 30410 Pte. T. LINDSAY of the CROSS ROAD'S FARM gun team being killed by a machine gun bullet. At Coy. HQ all the reserve teams and headquarters stood to arms. The alarm Gas & Smoke Helmets were put on. Lt. K.R.G. BROWNE O.C. Company reported to Brigade.	

WAR DIARY or INTELLIGENCE SUMMARY

Army Form C. 2118

Place	Date	Hour	Summary of Events and Information	Remarks and references to Appendices
YSER CANAL BANK at C.25.A.5.5. (YPERLEE)	Aug 8th		Headquarters immediately afterwards. Reserve guns, belt boxes and gun equipment were got ready to move. The enemy bombardment continued for about an hour and was replied to by our Artillery. The order to carry on as usual was given about 12 midnight. It appears that the enemy discharged gas over the front of the 11th Brigade, who were on the left of the 12th and also on its front of the division on the right of the 12th Brigade. Both the 11th and 12th Brigades were relieving at the time of the gas attack. No gas however came over on the front of the 13th Brigade. The heavy bombardment of the front of the 13th Brigade was carried out simultaneously with the gas attack on the front of the 11th Brigade.	1k.
"	Aug 9th		Uneventful.	1k.
"	Aug 10th Aug 11th		1 O.R. joined the company from the Base Depot. All guns in the line relieved by 2 teams from Coy. H.Q. Uneventful.	1k.
"	Aug 12th		A wire was received from the 12th Brigade stating that 2/Lt R.K. McALPIN from the B.F. Machine Gun Company was assuming to join the company to Command it with the rank of Temporary Captain.	1k.

Army Form C. 2118

WAR DIARY or INTELLIGENCE SUMMARY
(Erase heading not required.)

Place	Date	Hour	Summary of Events and Information	Remarks and references to Appendices
YPERLEE CANAL BANK C.25.A.5.5	Aug 13th 14th		Uneventful	Ref. BELGIUM Sheet 28 N.W. 1/20,000 Edition 3.D
	15th 16th		Completed relief of 2 teams in the line by 2 teams from Coy. H.Q. Lt. H. BRADBURY, 2nd Royal Sussex Regt. and Machine Gun Corps and 2 Lt. J.E. HAMMOND, Machine Gun Corps, joined the company from GRANTHAM Machine Gun Training Centre.	
	17th		Received B.M. No 595 from 12th Brigade H.Q. to the effect that when the "GAS ALERT" is sent out from Brigade H.Q. it must not be taken off except under orders from Brigade H.Q.	
	18th		Co. of 11th M. Gun Company visited Coy H.Q. to arrange details of relief for night of 19th inst. Section officers of 11th Coy were shown gun positions in the line. Representative attended a Quartermaster's Conference at Divisional Kit Conference & discussed winter clothing School and the D.A.D.O.S. 1st Division supplies etc. with the A.A. & Q.M.G.	
	19th		Received Relief Orders 12th 16th de Order No 30 Relief orders cancelled. Received 12th Bde new Relief orders dated 19/8/16 to the effect that all units of the 12th Bde except the M.G. Coy would be relieved on the night of the 19th/20th M.G. Coy to be relieved on the night of the 20th/21st and to be under the command of the G.O.C. 115th (2nd) Brigade until they were relieved by the 115th Machine Gun Company.	

1875 Wt. W593/826 1,000,000 4/15 J.B.C. & A. A.D.S.S./Forms/C. 2118.

WAR DIARY
or
INTELLIGENCE SUMMARY
(Erase heading not required.)

Army Form C. 2118

Place	Date	Hour	Summary of Events and Information	Remarks and references to Appendices
YPER LEE CANAL BANK C.25.a.5.5.	Aug 20th		Company commander of the 115th Machine Gun Company visited Coy H.Q with reference to relief that night. Dispositions of the Company in the line were explained to him.	Ref. BELGIUM Sheet 28 NW 1/20000 Edn. 3.D
		1 p.m.	Lieut K.F. McALPIN 86th Machine Gun Coy joined and took over command of the Company with the temporary rank of Captain.	
		10 p.m.	Relieving Sections of 115th M.G Coy arrived. One guide per team going into position in the line was provided.	1t
			Relief complete. Company moved off independently to billets in POPERINGHE. Lieut McALPIN and Lieut BROWNE visited the H.Q. of the 8th Canadian Machine Gun Company on the COMINES CANAL yf. etc	
POPERINGHE	21st	3 a.m.	near BEDFORD HOUSE ref. I 26 a 9.4. to arrange details of forthcoming relief of 8th Canadian M.G Coy on the nights of the 22nd/23rd. and 23rd/24th. An extract from Routine Orders by Bryg. Gen. J.D. CROSBIE, Commanding 12th Infantry Brigadier- dated Aug 21st 1916 is the following:- "The G.O.C. in C. has under authority granted him by his Majesty the King, been pleased to award the following decoration:-	
			MILITARY CROSS	
			Lieut. K.R.G. BROWNE 3rd ESSEX Regt. att. 12th Machine Gun Company.	

WAR DIARY or INTELLIGENCE SUMMARY

Army Form C. 2118

Place	Date	Hour	Summary of Events and Information	Remarks and references to Appendices
POPERINGHE	Aug 22	2 pm	Cleaning up of guns apparents etc by Sections. Section officers of "A" and "B" Sections left POPERINGHE to visit the line held by the 8th Canadian M.G. Coy and take over trench stores before arrival of relieving Sections.	
		8.15 pm	Trans left POPERINGHE for the ASYLUM, YPRES containing "A" and "B" Sections Limbers went by road to the ASYLUM. 8th Canadian M.G. Coy Guides met Sections at the ASYLUM and took Sections to their respective positions. "A" Section to the Centre Sector B Section to the Right Sector. Lt J.E. HAMMOND took over duties of Transport officer from Lt ROGERS 8th Canadian	
	23rd	2 am	Relief complete. "A" and "B" Sections under orders of G.O.C. 8th Canadian Infantry Brigade until G.O.C. 12th Brigade takes over.	
		6.30 pm	"D" Section moved to Reserve billets in D Camp with the Transport.	
		8.30 pm	"C" Section and Coy. H.Q. left POPERINGHE Station for ASYLUM. YPRES were met by Guides of the 8th Canadian M.G. Coy there.	
		12 Mid	Coy H.Q. arrived at 8th Canadian M.G. Coy H.Q. "C" Section went up to the line to relieve the left Section guns of 8th Can M.G. Coy	—
DUGOUTS ON COMINES— YPRES CANAL at I 25 C.	24th	3 am	Relief complete.	Ref BELGIUM Sheet 28 NW 20,000 Edition 3D.
		11.45 am	Capt K.F. McALPIN slightly wounded by Shrapnel and was evacuated to No. 10 C.C. Station. Lt K.R.G. BROWNE assumed command of Company.	
	25th		2 O.R. Wounded. (Shrapnel) G.O.C. 12th Inf. Brigade visited the guns in the line.	

Army Form C. 2118.

WAR DIARY
or
INTELLIGENCE SUMMARY.
(Erase heading not required.)

Place	Date	Hour	Summary of Events and Information	Remarks and references to Appendices
TRENCHES Coy H.Q. at I.25.c on YPRES-COMINES CANAL	Aug 2.6.		Sufficient time having now elapsed since the company took over the line, the dispositions of the Machine Guns in the line may now be given — (I) GENERAL 12 guns in position (3 Sections) and 4 guns / Sect in Reserve at Transport Lines in Sq. G.8.b. near POPERINGHE. The 4 Reserve guns carried on with ordinary Machine Gun training and also provided reliefs for the Sections in trenches (II) SPECIAL The sector held by the Brigade was divided into 3 — its left centre and right sectors each containing 4 guns. The line held by the 12th Brigade extended from ZILLEBEKE – KLEIN ZILLEBEKE road on the left Pt. I.29.d.I.7. to a point where the British line crossed the YPRES-COMINES. CANAL (at the BLUFF) on the right Pt. O.4.a 7.9. The main line of defence was the 3rd or Reserve line of the front line system of trenches the actual front line and support lines being held by a series of posts. Behind this ran another line of defence running from the YPRES-COMINES CANAL at Pt. I 33.a 3.7 in a North Easterly direction. In this line were 3 strong points. (I) No 7 Strong point at LA CHAPELLE Fm Pt I.33.b.4.9½	Ref. Trench Map BELGIUM Sheet 28NW Section 3D 1/20,000 Ref. SECRET Map N° K 37. of 8th Can. Inf. Bde dated 15.8.16.

Army Form C. 2118.

WAR DIARY
or
INTELLIGENCE SUMMARY.
(Erase heading not required.)

Instructions regarding War Diaries and Intelligence Summaries are contained in F. S. Regs., Part II. and the Staff Manual respectively. Title pages will be prepared in manuscript.

Place	Date	Hour	Summary of Events and Information	Remarks and references to Appendices
TRENCHES	Aug 26		(2) No 8 Strong Point at Pt I 28 c 5.0. (3) No 9 Strong Point at Pt I 28 d 3.8. The positions of the guns were as follows:-	Ref. Secret M.J. N? K.37 8th Canadian Inf. Brigade dated 16.8.16.
			(A) Left Sector.	
			Position (i) THE DUMP I 29 c 2½.3½. Covered from Hill 60 to right of Trench 39	
			(ii) CRESCENT TRENCH I 29 c 1.1. Covered front line from Railway to right of Trench 37.	
			(iii) VERBRANDENMOLEN I 28 d 4.4½. Covered from Railway to Trench 35	
			(iv) I 28 d 4.4. Swept ground from GRAND FLEET ST. to west of Trenches 38 exactly right of SUNKEN ROAD	
			(b) Centre Sector.	
			(v) GRAND FLEET ST. I 34 b 7.8. covered ground from top of ridge in VERBRANDEN MOLEN to Rear of Trenches 38 and 37.	
			(vi) 36 Suffolk I 34 b 8.6½. Covered rear of Trench 36 and part of 35.	
			(vii) Strong Point 8. I 28 c 7.1. Enfiladed SUNKEN ROAD and covered Reverse slopes of VERBRANDEN MOLEN	
			(viii) PETTICOAT LANE I 34 b 3½.5. Covered RAVINE.	
			(c) Right Sector	
			(ix) DAVIDSON LANE I 34 c 5.6 fired towards CRATER at Pt I 34 c 6.0.	
			(x) TUNNEL I 34 c D.1. fired along BLUFF and to left, crossing with No (x) gun	
			(xi) I 34 c 1.1 fired across CANAL + covered ground in front of Trenches 28 and 27 and on enemy front line opposite these trenches	
			(xii) GORDON POST I 33 d 1.8 covered ground behind Trenches 31 & 32 and also covered PEAR TREE WALK.	

Army Form C. 2118.

WAR DIARY
or
INTELLIGENCE SUMMARY.
(Erase heading not required.)

Instructions regarding War Diaries and Intelligence Summaries are contained in F.S. Regs., Part II. and the Staff Manual respectively. Title pages will be prepared in manuscript.

Place	Date August	Hour	Summary of Events and Information	Remarks and references to Appendices
TRENCHES	26th	5.55 p.m.	Enemy blew up a small mine at M I 29 c 7¼ 4. just to N. of Large Mine Crater at Hill 60. No damage was done.	Ref BELGIUM La Sheet 28. N.W. 3/8th 1:20,000
"	26th		Transport lines moved to Sqr G.8.b. (near POPERINGHE) from Sqr G 24 N.W. 3/8th about	
"	27th		Uneventful. hand for past 2 days. Varies from W. to S.W.	
"		15–20 m.p.h. air clear and good visibility obtainable.	
"	28th		Coy. Commander of M.G. Company Australian Forces visited Coy H.Q. to get particulars as to dispositions of Company in the trenches. "D" Section came up from Reserve at G.8.b. to relieve "C" Section in the Left Sector.	do
"		11.45 p.m	Relief complete in Left Sector.	
"	29th	10 am	Received copy of 12th Brie Order No 34 dated 29/8/16. The Brigade to be relieved by the 2nd Australian Brigade on the nights of the 30/31st Aug and 31/1 Sept.	
"		1 p.m.	Received 12th Bn. BM. 801 dated 29/8/16. with orders for operations by 12th M.Gun Company during the bombardment of the enemy lines opposite the 13th Bn. front from Pt I 30 c 9.9 to T 19 C 2.8. While the Artillery bombardment was going on Machine Guns of the Company were to enfilade with indirect fire the enemy's support trenches in Sq. I 30 C and area in neighbourhood of KLEIN ZILLEBEKE.	Ref Trench Map Belgium Sheet 28 N.W. & N.E. 1:20000 Edition 3 D

2353 Wt. W2344/1454 700,000 5/15 D.D.&L. A.D.S.S./Forms/C. 2118.

Army Form C. 2118.

WAR DIARY
or
INTELLIGENCE SUMMARY.
(Erase heading not required.)

Instructions regarding War Diaries and Intelligence Summaries are contained in F. S. Regs., Part II. and the Staff Manual respectively. Title pages will be prepared in manuscript.

Place	Date	Hour	Summary of Events and Information	Remarks and references to Appendices
TRENCHES	August 29th		Artillery bombardment was timed to take place between 3 pm and 4 pm.	
		3.15pm	2 Machine Guns opened fire as required but artillery bombardment did not take place.	
			During the day officers of the 2nd Australian Brigade Machine Gun Company visited gun positions in the line.	
		10.30pm	Alarm heard on the right of the Brigade coming from the direction of ST. ELOI. The alarm was taken up all round and all minutes immediately Stood to built. Smoke helmets on. The wind was blowing from 2-5 m/hr from a South Easterly direction. No rattling or infantry action of any kind followed.	
		11.15pm	Received messages from Brigade saying that the G.O.C. was not on duty Brigade front. The order Stand down was given.	b
	30th		Very heavy rains during the day. The Amn. Section in Right Sector was relieved by a section from the 2nd Australian Machine Gun Company.	b
	31st	3.25am	Relief complete in Right Sector.	
		11 pm	Left and Centre Sector Guns relieved by 2 sections of 2nd Australian Machine Gun Company. 4 O.R. joined the Company from M.G. Corps Base Depot.	b

4th Division
War Diaries
12th Infantry Bde
M. G. Coy.
September 3rd December
1916

12th Brigade.
4th Division.

12th INFANTRY BRIGADE

MACHINE GUN COMPANY

SEPTEMBER 1916

WAR DIARY
or
INTELLIGENCE SUMMARY.

(Erase heading not required.)

Army Form C. 2118.

Instructions regarding War Diaries and Intelligence Summaries are contained in F. S. Regs., Part II. and the Staff Manual respectively. Title pages will be prepared in manuscript.

Place	Date	Hour	Summary of Events and Information	Remarks and references to Appendices
HOUTPOUTRE SIDING near POPERINGHE	Sept 17th	1.30am	Train with Company left HOUTPOUTRE Station	Ref. France Sheet 14 Amiens
		11.30am	Train arrived at SALEUX near AMIENS.	
		1.30am	Company marched off from SALEUX less 2 sections left for detraining purposes.	
		4.30pm	Company arrived at RAINNEVILLE and went into billets	
		11.45pm	Detraining party of 2 sections arrived	
	18th		Lt ROBERTON rejoined Company from 2nd Army School. Lt ROGERS and 4 O.R. rejoined from 4th Divisional School.	W.D.R.
	19th		Uneventful	W.D.R.
	20th	10 P.M.	Inspection of Company Horses & Transport by Divisional Commander. Gun Mounting and Dismounting I.O.R. to M.G. Rums.	W.D.R.
	21st		I.O.R to M.S. Base underage. O.i/c gave lecture gas awelmets to all officers + N.C.Os on the new Small Box Respirator.	W.D.R
	22nd		Received order to return all men surplus to Establishment	W.D.R

WAR DIARY
or
~~INTELLIGENCE SUMMARY.~~

Army Form C. 2118.

Place	Date Sept	Hour	Summary of Events and Information	Remarks and references to Appendices
TRENCHES	1st	1.15 am	Relief reported complete in both sectors.	
		3 am	A & D sections and Coy HQ left the ASYLUM YPRES by train.	
		4.15 am	arrived POPERINGHE and proceeded to billets.	
			Received copy of wire from VIIIth Corps. "2nd Lt. R.R.G. BROWNE to command No. 212 machine gun company and to be temporary Captain whilst so employed". Lt. W. E. ROBERTON to be 2nd in command."	
	2nd	1.30 pm	Received 12th Bde Order No. 35 dated 2/9/16. "2 Sections of Bde. M.G. Coy to proceed to ELVERDINGHE to form the permanent garrison of that place. 1s. garrison of 8 machine guns. 1 officer and 50 O.R. to be attached to the 1st King's Own Regt. for training and work from 4/9/16.	
	3rd		The town of POPERINGHE was shelled during the morning and the company was moved out into the open country outside the town as per 12th Bde. B.M. 1 O.R. joined the company for duty. 2 from the 2nd Essex Regt and 5 from the 2nd Duke of Wellingtons Regt. These men were to be attached to learn machine gun work and generally assist in the work of the company.	

WAR DIARY
or
INTELLIGENCE SUMMARY.

Army Form C. 2118.

Place	Date	Hour	Summary of Events and Information	Remarks and references to Appendices
POPERINGHE	Sept 4th	7.30 a.m.	2 Sections "C" and "D" marched off to relieve the sections of the 114th Machine Gun Company on permanent machine gun garrison at ELVERDINGHE BELGIUM to be under the orders of the O.C. Battalion forming K. garrison of that place and to be made use of for training and work	Ref BELGIUM Sheet 28 N.W. 1:100,000.
		10.30 am	Relief complete at ELVERDINGHE	
		8 am	1 officer and 50 O.R. marched up to be attached to the 1st King's Own Regt. at BRANDHOEK Camp for training and work. Coy H.Q. and transport remained in POPERINGHE.	
"	5th		Uneventful.	
	6th		2nd Lt R.S. GEDDES and 1 N.C.O. left to join 4th Divisional School of Instruction for a course. 19 O.R. joined the company from M.G. Corps Base Depot.	
	7th		Uneventful.	
	8th		Received copy of 12th Inf. Brigade Defence Scheme while in Corps Reserve (Forward Brigade) dated 7/9/16. In case of attack the Company had to move to CAMP "N" at F.21.c with 1st line Transport: the sections with the Company had to garrison while the sections with the 1st King's Own have to rejoin the company in POPERINGHE and go with them to CAMP "N".	Ref BELGIUM 27 & 28 1/40,000

Army Form C. 2118.

WAR DIARY
or
INTELLIGENCE SUMMARY.
(Erase heading not required.)

Instructions regarding War Diaries and Intelligence Summaries are contained in F. S. Regs., Part II. and the Staff Manual respectively. Title pages will be prepared in manuscript.

Place	Date	Hour	Summary of Events and Information	Remarks and references to Appendices
POPERINGHE	Sept 9th		Uneventful.	
"	10th		Lt ROBERTON proceeded on a course to 2nd ARMY School. 63 O.R. joined from M.G. Corps Base Depot. G.O.C. 4th Inf. Brigade inspected draft of 63 O.R. who arrived on 10th inst.	
"	11th		Uneventful	
"	12th		Lt E. ROGERS and 4 O.R. proceeded on a course of Bayonet Fighting at the 4th Divisional School.	
"	13th			
"	14th		Uneventful	
"	15th			
"	16th	9.a.m	Received 4th DIV Q.R. 1320 orders for the Brigade to entrain and move	
		4pm	Sections A + B under Lt RAY rejoined from being attached to the 15th King's Own.	
		9pm	2 Sections garrisoning EWERDINGHE rejoined Company in POPERINGHE	
		11.15pm	Company marched off from POPERINGHE to entraining point	

Army Form C. 2118.

WAR DIARY
or
INTELLIGENCE SUMMARY.

(Erase heading not required.)

Instructions regarding War Diaries and Intelligence Summaries are contained in F. S. Regs., Part II. and the Staff Manual respectively. Title pages will be prepared in manuscript.

Place	Date	Hour	Summary of Events and Information	Remarks and references to Appendices
RANNEVILLE.	23rd	8 A.M.	4/9 O.R. to M.G. Base Depot aeroplus to Establishment. Lt. Straight conducting their.	WER
	27	3.30 P.M.	2/Lt STRAIGHT + Sgt BECKER to Machine Gun Course CAMIERS.	WER
	24th	8 A.M.	Received D.M.A.S.9. from 18th Brigade.	
			Received B.M. 161 from 12th Brigade; "Nabs on reconnaissances of troops in the Somme Battle"	WER
			Received 12th Bde Order No 36 B/M 5 on 1st march attd Herbst	
	25th	3 P.M.	Company marched off at 3 P.M. to ALLONVILLE via pointonists. Arrived at new billets 3-40 P.M. Sell into line of march nil. - Coy HQ de Burlengers Rue des Anges.	WER
ALLONVILLE	26th	10.30 A.M.	Company left ALLONVILLE and marched to LA NEUVILLE via PIERRIES. Arrived at new billets 1 P.M.:- Fell out on march nil:- Coy HQ at No 2 Rue Rue de Pickets.	WER
LA NEUVILLE	27th 28th		Company carried out Bde training. Otherwise nonentful.	WER
			1 O.R. to Base underage. Training soon on 27th. Received 2 copies of XIV Corps Circs.	WER
	29.	4-45 A.M.	2/Lt LIGHTBODY + 4 O.R. to R.F.C No 9 Squadron to practise communication with Contact Aeroplane Patrol.	WER
			Conference at Bde HQ of all C.Os with G.O.C.	WER

2353 Wt. W2544/1454 700,000 5/15 D. D. & L. A.D.S.S./Forms/C. 2118.

Army Form C. 2118.

WAR DIARY
or
INTELLIGENCE SUMMARY.

(Erase heading not required.)

Instructions regarding War Diaries and Intelligence Summaries are contained in F. S. Regs., Part II. and the Staff Manual respectively. Title pages will be prepared in manuscript.

Place	Date	Hour	Summary of Events and Information	Remarks and references to Appendices
LA NEUVILLE	30th		Bomb training. 2/Lt. J. LIGHTBODY & A.O.P. returned from 9th Squadron R.F.C.	WCR
		9-0 P.M.	Night Operations	

12th Brigade.

4th Division.

12th INFANTRY BRIGADE

MACHINE GUN COMPANY

OCTOBER 1 9 1 6

Attached :- Reports on Operations 12th & 23rd October

Army Form C. 2118.

WAR DIARY
or
INTELLIGENCE SUMMARY.
(Erase heading not required.)

Instructions regarding War Diaries and Intelligence Summaries are contained in F.S. Regs., Part II. and the Staff Manual respectively. Title pages will be prepared in manuscript.

Place	Date 1916	Hour	Summary of Events and Information	Remarks and references to Appendices
LA NEUVILLE	1st Oct.	1. A.M.	Summer Time altered to Winter Time. Church Parade at 11-30 A.M.	WR 3
"	2nd Oct.		Uneventful. Brigade Training carried out.	WR 4
"	3rd Oct.	3 P.M.	2/Lt. R.S. GEDDES & 2. O.R. rejoined from the 4th Div School.	WR 5
	4 Oct		Uneventful. Received a copy of orders from appointments, Commanding, etc. No 105. Transferring 2/Lt. E. ROGERS 2 Paris Fusiliers and 2/Lt. R.M. STRAIGHT Essex Regiment each to this Machine Gun Corps to date with 12 Company, to fill establishment, and date from 26th January 1916.	WR 6
	5 Oct		Usual training during the morning. Company bathed in the afternoon at Baths in CORBIE	WR 7
	6 Oct.	6-10 AM	Orders issued for B.C. Scheme practice attack on FRANVILLERS on the 6th inst. Secret Orders received from Bde. Company paraded 8 A.M. & marched off 8-15 A.M. via LA HOUSSAYE and P.P. 122 to the assembly position for the B.C. Practice attack on FRANVILLERS. The assembly position for Coy H.Q and reserve guns was near C.21 d 1. The attack started 11-15 A.M. & operations were concluded about 1-30 P.M. The company then marched to date to tableto.	Ref Sheet 62 D.N.W. 20,000

Army Form C. 2118.

WAR DIARY
or
INTELLIGENCE SUMMARY.
(Erase heading not required.)

Instructions regarding War Diaries and Intelligence Summaries are contained in F.S. Regs., Part II. and the Staff Manual respectively. Title pages will be prepared in manuscript.

Place	Date	Hour	Summary of Events and Information	Remarks and references to Appendices
LANEUVILLE	6 Oct 1916	6.10 P.M.	Received 12th Bde Operation Order No 38 for move into CORBIE on 7th inst. These were cancelled 10 P.M.	W.S.R.
	7 Oct	7.30 A.M.	2/Lt POGERS & 2 O.R. proceeded on a course of instruction to 4th Divisional School. 12th Bde Operation Order No 39 Copy No 5 received this morning.	
		9.10 P.M.	Amendment to 12th Bde Order No 39 Copy No 5 :——— Bde H.Q. March W.D. Copy No 1 and 12th Bde No Q.C. 251.	
	8th		9/Lt FRIGHTER & Sgt GLENN to report to 16th & M.G. Co. to take over line. Company left LANEUVILLE on the morning of 8th inst. to proceed to CITADEL CAMP (F.21.c) 9/Lt GEDDES & C.Q.M.S. Roberts advance billeting party.	
CITADEL CAMP			Arrived CITADEL CAMP 3.30 P.M. ——— 1 O.R. fell out & admitted to Hospital. Received Bde Operation Orders at 11.30 P.M. (D.O. No 40)	Ref Map Sheet 1/100,000 ALBERT 1/20,000 Sheet 57d S.W.
	9th	8.15 A.M.	Company marched off to the line at 8.15 A.M. ——— 2/Lt HAMMOND was sent forward to reconnoitre routes for transport. Much bomb for Company :—— FRICOURT Cemetery — Link R.P.F.P.C.S.W. — Road through Knoll — T8 Central. March Route for Company :— HAMEL 72 — MONTAUBAN — GUILLEMONT — GINCHY — destination. T8 Central. Arrived T.8 Central about 1.30 P.M. & took guides from 16th M.G. Coy.	

WAR DIARY
or
INTELLIGENCE SUMMARY.

(Erase heading not required.)

Army Form C. 2118.

Place	Date	Hour	Summary of Events and Information	Remarks and references to Appendices
	9th	11.30PM	Transport arrived Company H.Q. near GUILLEMONT — 2 limbers lost	1 WR
	10th	2.30 A.M.	A and C Sections started off for relief at about 12.30 P.M.	
		2.30 A.M.	2/Lt R.S. GEDDES killed by a shell, also 3 guides of 16th U Coy + 15 officer guide severely wounded. A + C Sections left wounded to be evacuated + returned to T.B. Central to try + get in touch with Coy H.Q. to find guides. It was too late to continue so relief was postponed till evening of 11th & all were told guides would meet Sections at T.2. Central — Rat hunting	
		5.30 P.M	Guides met A+C Sections T.B. Central & relief was continued	WR
	10th		Capt. BROWNE admitted to Hospital and 1 O.R. killed	
	11th		Secret Orders re Trenches received — 10.R. wounded	
			Secret Orial Report LE TRANSLOY received	
	11. 12th	3.30 A.M.	Relief of Coy until 166th Coy officially notified complete.	
			48 O.R. attached to Coy from — Batts. — 20 R. to hospital	
			Secret Orders re new Zero hour received from Batts. also Dart Pamphlet.	1 WR
	12th	11.0 A.M.	Coy H.Q. moved to dug-out with ESSEX H.Q. at T.8 Central for the above Attack. 2/Lt BRADBURY left in charge of transport. Water bottles none S.24.6.9.4.	

WAR DIARY
INTELLIGENCE SUMMARY
(Erase heading not required.)

Army Form C. 2118.

Place	Date	Hour	Summary of Events and Information	Remarks and references to Appendices
Trenches	12th	2.5 P.M.	Sgt. McManus + 1th reserve men moved to BERNAFAY WOOD. ZERO HOUR. Operations Commenced. — Artillery Barrage fire for ½ an hour during which infantry made the assault.	See APPENDIX Nº IA
		9.0 P.M.	Received word 2/Lt. RAY wounded & reinforcements required.	APPENDIX IA Page 6 Para (1), (2).
		10.30 P.M.	Received message 2/Lt. FRICKER wounded & his reinforcements required. Unofficial Casualties — Sgt. Ray, Bibbs + L/Cpl. Camp wounded. Reserve men sent up to reinforce position in line under 2/Lt. LIGHTBODY. 2/Lt. BRADBURY came up to take 2/Lt. LIGHTBODY's place at Coy. H.Q.'s Central.	
	13th		Received report 1 gun put out of action. Number of casualties not yet verified. Total number of available Gun Teams : - 2/Lieut. R.S. GEDDES killed 10th inst. 2/Lieut. FRICKER wounded 12th inst. and 2/Lieut. RAY missing believed wounded 12th inst. — 7 O.R. killed and 8 O.R. wounded.	(W.O.R.)
		5 P.M.	"D" Section fell in & proceeded to relieve "C" Section and remainder of "A" Section under 2/Lieut. J. BRADBURY.	(W.O.R.)
	14th		Relief of above effected in the early morning.	(W.O.R.)
	15th		2 O.R. wounded. — 9/Lieut. STRAIGHT & 2 O.R. rejoined from M.G. School CAMIERS.	(W.O.R.)

WAR DIARY
or
INTELLIGENCE SUMMARY.
(Erase heading not required.)

Army Form C. 2118.

Place	Date	Hour	Summary of Events and Information	Remarks and references to Appendices
Trenches	15th		2/Lieut. W.J.H. GRAINGER joined the Company from GRANTHAM.	WSR
	16th		"C" Section relieved "B" Section. — Disposition of Company, 1st Army "D" Section and 2 teams of "C" Section in the Line, — 1 team "C" in Reserve GERMAN Dug Out and 1 Team "C" Section in Reserve T.S. Central; — A & B Sections in Brigade Reserve at Coy H.Q. S.24.b.9.4. — 28th Reinforcements at TRÔNES WOOD. Received information of new C.O. for C/65 Company, also multiplication of Officers of 20 O.R. Reinforcements.	
			G.O.C. Bde. interviewed O.C. Company re: Operations for the 16th inst. — 2/Lt GRAINGER	WSR
	17th		2/Lt STRAIGHT relieved 2/Lt BRADBURY in the Line. Proceeded to TRÔNES WOOD to join 28th Reinforcements	
		3.45 LIGHTBODY	returned to Coy H.Q. S.24.b.9.4. Orders received from Bde. for Operations of 18th inst, & refillable with Company Operation Orders by O.C. Company. — O.C. too returned to T.S. Central, WR Rm (71 & 3) Operations Commenced.	See Appendix 338 Para I APPENDIX IIIA
	18th	3.40 A.M	ZERO HOUR; — Operations Commenced: — During operations T6 Central reported shelled with H.E. and Lachrymatory Shells. 1 O.R. wounded.	WSR

WAR DIARY
or
INTELLIGENCE SUMMARY.
(Erase heading not required.)

Army Form C. 2118.

Place	Date	Hour	Summary of Events and Information	Remarks and references to Appendices
	18th		In the morning Coy. H.Q removed from 78 Central to S24 b.9.n. — C.O. interviewed G.O.C re relief.	
	19th	11.30 P.M	Secret Operation Orders re Relief received Officer of 23rd M.G. Coy visited Coy H.Q to take over part of line.	
	20th		2/Lt LENSK + 2/Lieut TOSE joined Coy H.Q. also 2 O.R. STRONGS WOOD. Relief of Sections. At B relieved C & D. Part of Company, via left Sector relieved by 23rd M.G. Coy viz 2 3rd M.G. Coy relieved 'C' Section. 12th Company took over rest of our Sub Coy 11th Company viz 'B' Section relieved 1 Section of 11th Company. A Section relieved. Instead that relieves of 'D' Section.	
	31st	10.0 A.M	Relief with 23rd Coy officially reported complete. Relief in morning received official word from 2/Lt 116th Body that relief of B Section and 11th Company now complete. Secret Operation Orders for 23rd received.	

WAR DIARY
or
INTELLIGENCE SUMMARY.
(Erase heading not required.)

Army Form C. 2118.

Place	Date	Hour	Summary of Events and Information	Remarks and references to Appendices
	23rd		2/Lt F. COMERY joined the Company from GRANTHAM. Amendment to Operation Orders received.	W.R
	22nd		Reinforcements from TROYES WOOD auk[illegible] to Coy. H.Q. Coy. H.Q. moved to T.5 Central in the afternoon. Special Company Orders issued under "Operation Orders" for 23rd inst.	See Appendix III B Ref. to Para 1 ORDERS W.R
	23rd	9.0 A.M	ZERO HOUR postponed from 11.30 A.M. to 2.30 P.M. on account of mist. Guns opened periodical outbursts of fire during mist.	APPENDIX III A and APPENDIX III B W.R
		2.30 P.M	ZERO HOUR and Operations commenced. 2nd Lt. R. wounded. ——— For account & report of Operations see Offensive [illegible]	W.R
	24th		Order to relieve Coy 95 I.B & M.G. Co received. O.C. 95th Company interviewed O.C. 12th Coy re arrangements for relief.	W.R
		5.30 P.M	Relief commenced; — greatly delayed owing to guides losing the way.	
	25th	3.50 A.M	Relief completed. — Company marched off. Relief at Coy H.Q. S.24.b.9.4. Rest [illegible] Lorries were parked. — Company marched to rest in area BERNAFAY WOOD	W.R

Army Form C. 2118.

WAR DIARY
or
INTELLIGENCE SUMMARY.
(Erase heading not required.)

Instructions regarding War Diaries and Intelligence Summaries are contained in F. S. Regs., Part II. and the Staff Manual respectively. Title pages will be prepared in manuscript.

Place	Date	Hour	Summary of Events and Information	Remarks and references to Appendices
	25th	10.30 a.m.	Departed from BERNAFAY WOOD for CITADEL CAMP. (F.21.b.) Route:- GUILLEMONT – MONTAUBAN – CARNOY Road and thence by Cross Country tracks to Camp. (F.21.b.)	Ref. Bn Order No 199
	26th	12.30 a.m.	Arrived at CITADEL CAMP.	
		9.15 a.m.	G.O.C. 4th Division presented medals to M.C.O.S. Men awarded medals.- C.S.M. WARD in elevated with rifle. 2nd Order of St George (Russia)	WCB
		10.15 a.m.	G.O.C. Div. had a conference at Bde. H.Q. with Commanding Officers of units & discussed recent operations	UCR
	27th		3/Lt HAMMOND & 1 O.R. to LE HAVRE for course of TRANSPORT duties 2/Lt LIGHTBODY proceed on leave to U.K.	
		2.30 p.m.	Bn fell in to march off to TREUX. - ref Report No. 50, Route :- To MEAULTE by main Road; (Cemetery Cross Road F.9.a) and thence by main Road to TREUX.	WCB
		6.30 p.m.	Company arrived at TREUX :- H.Q. No. 12 Billet.	
	28th		Uneventful:- received Movement order from Bde	
	29th	5.45 a.m.	Transport formed up and moved off to 1st Halting Place to night ARGOEUVES	

Army Form C. 2118.

WAR DIARY
or
INTELLIGENCE SUMMARY.
(Erase heading not required.)

Instructions regarding War Diaries and Intelligence Summaries are contained in F. S. Regs., Part II. and the Staff Manual respectively. Title pages will be prepared in manuscript.

Place	Date	Hour	Summary of Events and Information	Remarks and references to Appendices
	29.9	10.0 A.M.	Company less transport fell in and marched off to entraining station at MERICOURT L'ABBE. Siding.	
		12-0 NOON	Train moved off for AIRAINES.	
		2.30 P.M.	Transport arrived at ARQUEVRES and billeted for night.	Ref. Map Sheet 11 ABBEVILLE 100,000 W.E.R.
		10.30 P.M.	Arrived at detraining Station AIRAINES and company after detraining fell in and marched to WOIREL.	
	30.9	2-3 A.M.	Company arrived at Billets in WOIREL:— H.Q. at Chateau WOIREL.	Ref. Map DIEPPE 16 100,000 W.E.R
		8.0 A.M.	Transport departed ARQUEVRES and arrived Company Billets WOIREL 7-0 P.M.	W.E.R
	3.4		Uneventful.	W.E.R

Copy   SUG- APPENDIX

12th Infantry Brigade N° G.R. 263.

In order to compile a report on the operations carried out by the Division on the 12th, 18th, and 23rd inst the G.O.C. the Division wishes Commanders of Units to render reports on their part in the operations.

The Reports should include:—

(a) Orders.
(b) Important messages.
(c) Action of various Companys, Detachments, Machine Guns, Snipers, Bombers etc and result of these actions.
(d) Action of the enemy and results of enemy's Barrage.
(e) Remarks on:— Positions of Commanders in the attack, and suggestions.
   Equipment and method of carrying
   Feeding arrangements
   Assembly trenches
   Communication
   Artillery Support.

Signed
V. N. Johnson
Major
Brigade Major
12th Infantry Brigade

30th October 1916.

APPENDIX IA

12TH MACHINE GUN COMPANY.

Copy of Final Report on Co-operation of No 12. Machine Gun Company:- Operations of 12TH Oct. 1916
By
LIEUT. W.E. ROBERTON. Commanding 12TH Machine Gun Company

OPERATION ORDERS

Extract Bde O.O. No 41. Para 8. Machine Guns
The 2 guns allotted to assaulting Battalions will on the 1ST. Objective being captured be sent forward to check any counter attack.

As the further advance progresses one of these guns will be sent forward to the 2nd Objective

The 4 Special mission guns will put a barrage on the LE. TRANSLOY Cemetery Road commencing at ZERO hour.

They will also fire on the trenches at Pt N. 29.d.2.1. and N.29.c.9.4. until O+20 min when they will lift on to the trenches around the Cemetery South of the road and stop firing at O+30 min: when they will advance into SPECTRUM trench

The remaining 8 guns will await orders to move

Upon receipt of Operation Orders No 41. I had copies issued to Section Officers.
I allotted the Company as follows:-

1. Disposition
   ① 2 guns under Sgt BARRETT with 2/Lancs. Fusiliers } "A" Section
   ② 2 guns under 2 Lt C. L. KAY. with 2/Duke of Wellingtons }

   ③ 4 guns SPECIAL MISSION under 2/Lt W.L. FRICKER
                                                                           "C" Section.

   ④ 8 guns in reserve :- 'B' and 'D' Section.

I A

2. **Special Company Orders.**
The following additional orders were issued to Section Officers of A & C. Sections with copies of Bde Operation Orders on 11th Oct 1916.

a. <u>Equipment</u>: Fighting Order less Packs.

b. <u>Strength of Teams</u>: Teams will go into action as they are at present. When advancing they will move in file.

c. <u>Reserve Dump of S.A.A. for M.G. Company</u>
Dump for supply of S.A.A. for belt filling will be established near Lancs. Fusiliers Hd.Qrs. in SUNKEN. RD. A and D Sections will draw on that dump for belt filling purposes.

d. <u>Coy H.Q.</u> will be established at ESSEX. Battn HQ. at T.8.d 3.6. in the FLERS. line.
All reports from A & C. Sections will be sent there.

e. Section Officers of A Section will report to O.C. Lancs. Fusiliers and O.C. Dukes. to arrange the details of the advance with them.

f. <u>8 Picks and 8 Shovels</u> will be sent down to-night. One pick and one shovel per team are to be carried.

g. A Section will take 8 belt boxes per gun.

h. <u>All Packs</u> of A and C sections to be dumped at Section Officers dug-out.

i. Section Officers will synchronise their watches at Lancs Fusiliers Battn H.Q. at 9-30 p.m. 11th inst. and 11 a.m. 12th inst.

3. The 2 guns of B Section will remain in reserve at GERMAN. dug-out. Sgt Glenn will rejoin these 2 guns. This ½ Section will await orders from the C.O.

4. <u>Communication</u> There will be 2 runners at 2 Lieut FRICKER'S dug-out and 2 at GERMAN dug-out. These runners will work in relay to Coy H.Q. at T.8. central.

IA

3

4. Communication (Cont'd)

Any urgent message can be sent from Lancs Fusiliers Batt. H.Q. telephone to Coy H.Q. at T.8. central.

5. Carriers

On the 11th inst 48. O.R's. were attached to the Company as carriers for the Operations

They were disposed of as follows.

1. 12 O.R. from 2/Dukes of Wellingtons were attached to 'A' Section (3 per team)
2. 12 O.R. from Lancs Fusiliers to 'C' Section (3 per gun team)
3. 12 O.R. from Essex at advanced Coy H.Q. T.8. Central.
4. 12. O.R. from Kings Own. at Coy H.Q. near GUILLEMONT.

6. DUMPS for Supply of S.A.A.

The following special M.G. dumps were established

① FORWARD DUMP. N.34.c.2.9. near Lancs Fus H.Q. Sunken Rd:— 20,000. Rds
② RESERVE DUMP. GERMAN dug-out:— 28,000. Rds
③ With 8 Guns in line. (4,000 Rds per gun)
   32,000 Rds

Total 80,000 Rds

7. ASSEMBLY. POSITIONS

① Left. ½ 'A' Section under Sgt BARRETT in SPECTRUM with Lancs Fusiliers Company.
② Right. ½ 'A' Section under 2 Lieut C.L. KAY. in WINDY. TR. with Dukes Company.
③ Special Mission 'C' Section in positions in Square M.34.a. from the high ground behind the SUNKEN ROAD around WINDMILL. TR.
④ ½ 'B' and 'D' Sections in Reserve round Coy H.Q. near GUILLEMONT.
⑤ ½. B. Section under Sgt GLENN in immediate reserve at GERMAN dug-out

I A
4

- **OPERATIONS.**

  CATEGORY. (6) Bde G.R. 263. (See Sub-Appendix)

  During operations. I received the following important messages by telephone.

  ① (Received 12th inst about 9-0. p.m.)

  " 2 Lieut KAY. is a casualty AAA.
  1 Gun lost, shortage of belt boxes AAA
  please send reinforcements."

  FROM. 2 Lieut FRICKER
  'C' Section REFUGE. 7-30 p.m.

  ② About 10-30 p.m. I was called upon the phone from No 2. Bde relay post, and got following message.

  " Reinforcements required M.G. AAA.
  4 Guns under a L/Cpl and 10 men AAA
  They have no S.A.A. AAA. 2 Lt FRICKER
  wounded AAA"

  FROM. RECORD. 10-5 p.m.

  Regarding the action I took on receipt of above messages I refer you to my 1st report On Operations 12th Just sent you

  Written 1-20 PM. 13-10-16

  ESSEX Bn Hd Qrs

IA   5

6. **OPERATIONS.**

II Category (c) Bde G.R. 263. (See SUB APPENDIX)

<u>Action of 'C' Section. Special Mission.</u>

The Barrage indirect fire of C Section was carried out in accordance with 12TH Bde O.O. 41.

About 9,000 rds in all were fired by the 4 guns from ZERO hour until 0+30 min

After this the guns got ready to move forward to take up positions in SPECTRUM trench during the move, whilst 2 Lieut W. L. FRICKER and Sgt RAY were organising the team a shell wounded the former and killed the latter. The Section was thus left without a Senior N.C.O. of any kind.

Unfortunately evidence shows that 2 Lieut FRICKER was hit before he had given instructions to his team commanders, exactly how they were to proceed to SPECTRUM trench and what part they were to take up positions. However L/Cpl BUTLER took the initiative and endeavoured to get into touch with H.Q.

He went and reported to the O.C. Lanc Fusiliers for instructions. He was told to keep the section where it was until the O.C. Lancs Fusiliers got into touch with O.C. Machine Gun Coy. I then received important message (see para 6 Operations Heading 1. Sub head 2. Page 3)

Prior to receiving this message I had already sent forward 2 Lieut. J. LIGHTBODY with ½ 'B' Section as reinforcements.

On his arrival there, SUNKEN Rd. he found L/Cpl BUTLER and 'C' Section, so he assumed Command.

IA

When he (2ⁿᵈ Lieut. LIGHTBODY) got information about the situation from O.C. Lancs Fus he placed 2 Guns of 'B' Section in THISTLE. TRENCH and 1 gun of C. Section in the new Strong Pt near CURRIE. TR.

The remaining 3 guns of 'C' Section he left in reserve near by him to be disposed of later when he had got more information as to the tactical situation

---

B. <u>Action of A. Section</u>

Ⓐ left ½ Section 2 guns with Lancs Fusiliers in SPECTRUM. TRENCH. under Sgt. BARRETT.

In accordance with O.O 41. the ½ Section was not to go forward until 1st. Objective had been captured

Sgt BARRETT. states that he could not get any information whether the 1st Objective had been taken or not so he remained in Assembly positions

Ⓑ Right ½ Section in WINDY. TRENCH. with Company of Duke of Wellingtons

Information received from L/c Fairhall i/c No 4 Team

1. He went across towards the 1st Objective to take up positions there by 2 Lt KAY'S orders.
2. He got into a position at the junction of SPECTRUM. and DEWDROP. TR. near M34.d.8.
3. <u>His team got scattered crossing so he had to gather together a team in DEWDROP where he mounted his gun about M 34. d 8.</u>
4. Near by was a German Machine Gun which had been abandoned by its team who had evidently removed the feed block so as to render it useless
5. He found that the trench had not been properly cleared by the Dukes and that the Germans were in the same trench about 70 yds to the right

I A

6.(Cont᠎d) Meanwhile the Dukes had gone forward towards their 2nd Objective leaving about 25 men in the piece of trench he was in.

7. He saw 2 Lieut KAY. go forward with the Dukes between his team and No 3 team which was about 100 yds to the left of No 4.

8. Later 2 Lieut KAY was reported wounded whilst advancing and was missing. L/C Fairhall made several efforts to find him but did not succeed.

9. The party of Dukes in the trench had meanwhile erected a barricade between them and the Germans.

10. L/Cpl Fairhall then moved his gun to a more commanding position from which he could repel any counter attack

11. He remained in this trench all night and following day. This party was evidently cut off from the remainder of the Dukes.

12. On the evening of the 13th inst about 5-45.P.M. the Germans started to come across on the right. He opened fire and stopped them, and repelled repeated efforts of small parties to advance: he states he fired in all about 2 Belts.

13. About 10 P.M. 13th they got into communication with the Company in rear who were evidently sapping towards them and when the small party of Dukes were relieved he went out with them and eventually reported to 2 Lt LIGHTBODY in SUNKEN RD. and was sent back into reserve.

Ref Trench Map Sheet 57°S.W. 1/20,000   APPENDIX II A.

Copy of Report on Co-operation of No
12 Machine Gun Company :- Operations 18th Oct.
By
Lieut. W. E. Roberton.
Comdg. No 12 Machine Gun Company.

Sent to No 12 Inf Brigade 19th Oct.

1. 2 guns in SPECTRUM TRENCH

   A. The Right gun under L/Cpl Melhuis did good work & fired off about 1750 Rounds Traversing fire on ZENITH Trench.

   B. The Left gun unfortunately was knocked off the parapet and buried after it had just opened fire by a large H.E. Shell. Most of the team were buried but fortunately no one was wounded. The gun was not damaged but so caked with mud that it was impossible to fire it at all.

2. Special Mission Guns :- Indirect Fire Barrage.

   Up to the present I have had no report from the infantry as to the effect of the Indirect Barrage Fire.

   The firing was on the whole good the superintending officer informs me, but several stoppages occurred.

   The bullets appeared to be going well over the heads of our own troops.

   Owing to some of the stoppages being of a prolonged nature the number of rounds expended was not so great as

II A

expected, but nearly 6,000 rounds in all were fired in rapid bursts from ZERO hour to 0+ 30 min.

3. The guns doing the Indirect Fire were not heavily shelled. H.E Shrapnel was continually falling over the area occupied by them.

The 2 guns in the front line were not picked out as special targets, but the whole trench was continually shelled by heavy H.E Shells.

Special Notes

1. Owing to bad climatic conditions & the fact that it had to be done under cover of darkness great difficulty was experienced in laying & setting the Special Mission guns for Indirect Fire.

2. Stoppages :— No 1. gun had a prolonged stoppage caused by a broken fusee spring.

No 3 gun ran out of water but was able to continue firing by borrowing some from No 2 gun.

Owing to the muddy state of the trenches & heavy rain a number of minor stoppages occurred due to dirt getting into Breech Casings.

W.E Roberton Lieut.
O.C Company

Trench Map Sheet 57°S.W. 1/20,000. **APPENDIX II B**

3

Copy of Final Report sent to 12th Inf. Brigade.
on
CO-OPERATION of MACHINE GUNS on OPERATIONS 18th Oct
By
LIEUT. W. E. ROBERTON.
Comdg No 2 Machine Gun Company

1. Category (a) Bde G.R. 263 (See Sub-Appendix)

ORDERS.

(i) Ref Bde O.O. No 43 Para 6 Machine Gun Company

(ii) Special Orders by O.C. Company for
BARRAGE FIRE.

(a) Limits of Barrage.
Left Limit :— Line drawn thro'
N 29 a 0.0 to N 29 Central.

Right Limit :— Line thro' N 35 c.0.5. to
N 35 d.0.5.

(b) Special Note :— No 1 gun will
cross fire to the right and will
put up Right Limit of Barrage fire.
This gun must not fire to the right
past a Bearing of 93° True.
Set gun 93° T.B. and traverse 15° Left
Range 2000ˣ

(c) No 2 (Centre) gun :— at N 33 d 4.2 will
fire on X Rds CEMETERY Circle —
SUNKEN Rᴅ LE-TRANSLOY
N 35 b 3½ 28½
Range 2000ˣ enfilade fire.

(d) No 3 Right gun :— will fire and sweep ground
and trenches from Left limit of
Traverse, i.e. 35° T.B traversing 13° Right

(e) No 4 gun (Supplementary) at position near
Centre gun will fire at X Rds N 35 b 1.8.

(f) No 5 gun (Supplementary) at position mid-way
between Left + Centre guns will fire on
Approx Bearing of 50° true — Traverse 25° Right

II B

(g) <u>Casualties</u>. will be reported to Coy H.Q. 78 Central (ie Dukes H.Q).

Estimated Casualties could be reported by telephone to O.C. Company at 3rd, 6th, 9th and 14th hrs after ZERO.

Verified return of casualties should be sent by runner whenever possible.

(h) <u>Reports in Writing</u> as to the situation and expenditure of rounds should be sent by runner at 1½, 3, 4½ and 6 hours after ZERO.

---

2. <u>REPORT ON OPERATIONS</u>
Category (e) Bde GR 263 (see SUB APPENDIX)

Action of:-

A. 2 guns in SPECTRUM TRENCH.

B. Special Mission Guns; Indirect Fire Barrage

Reference above I refer you to my "Report on Co-operation of No 12 Machine Gun Company — Operations 18th Oct."

APPENDIX III A.

Copy of Report sent to 12th Inf Bde
By Lieut W.E. ROBERTON
Comdg No 12 Machine Gun Company

REPORT ON OPERATIONS 23rd inst.

I. 6 guns INDIRECT FIRE.
   Supervising Officers 2Lt Bradbury & Lt Leask

A. Statement of Report received from 2Lt Bradbury.
   1. At ZERO the 6 guns opened fire on the line N35 D 5.5 to N35 A 8.8 till ZERO + 8 minutes.
   2. At ZERO + 8 mins they sighted to 2.500 & opened fire on CEMETERY and SUNKEN Rd about N35.a
   3. They ceased fire at ZERO + 35 MIN
   During the morning fog, in accordance with orders received, they fired occasional bursts at the first targets.

B. Firing Report
   1. N° 12 TEAM was only able to fire 250 rounds in the ½ hour, occasioned by a broken fusee spring.
   2. Right Gun fired 8 belt boxes, 2000 rounds. No stoppages.
   3. Centre Gun fired 500 rounds then had a broken Muzzle-cup.
   4. N° 4 gun did well. Fired 2250 rounds. 2 minor stoppages.
   5. Left Gun fired 2050 rounds. 1 broken lock spring & a new belt caused several N°1 stoppages.
   6. N° 11 Team fired 2000 rounds & had a few ordinary stoppages.
   7. TOTAL number of Rounds fired during ZERO + 35 Min = 9050 Rounds.

   Sgt Channer who was in our Front Line during firing stated they put up a very good Barrage fire, & bullets appeared to pass well over the heads of our Infantry.
   1 O.R. wounded during Operations.

III A

Remarks on Stoppages by O.C. Company.

1. The wear & tear on guns during INDIRECT FIRE for a prolonged period is heavy & stoppages are bound to occur.

2. Owing to the fact that the weather was frosty, we experienced great difficulty, by the oil becoming cloggy, thus causing temporary stoppages.
   A mixture of paraffin with oil prevents this to a great extent, unfortunately, we have not received an issue although we have indented for same.

B. Report on work of 2 guns under Sgt Channer in SPECTRUM TRENCH.

Summary of statement made by Sgt Channer who was wounded shortly after commencement of operations.

He states both guns in SPECTRUM fired & had good targets for a short time on the enemy who were seen retiring from one of their trenches in rear of DEWDROP system. This was confirmed later by a report from 2/Lt Lightbody.

When Sgt Channer left his ½ Section in charge of Cpl. Fay the guns were still in Assembly positions.

2/Lt Lightbody issued instructions to Cpl. Fay to remain there until further orders. The guns were therefore not sent forward as our infantry apparently had not taken 1st Objective.

The ½ Section remained in SPECTRUM during night 23/24th.

During morning of 24th I received a further report from 2/Lt Lightbody asking me for instructions to withdraw these guns & put one in its old defensive position in THISTLE & the other in a position adjoining his HQ in SUNKEN RD. I therefore sent back word telling him to do that.

Casualties during Operations.

1 Sgt & 1 OR. wounded.

III A

O.C. Company's remarks.

1. Great difficulty in getting reliable information through - re the situation.
2. It was nearly 3 hours before I received the first report from my own people.
3. After that I received reports from my own Section Officers fairly regularly.
4. Section Officers in the line had the greatest of difficulty in getting any information as to progress of our infantry.
5. My own Relay system of runners from my Section Officers' H Q in the line to my own H Q T8 Central worked admirably.
6. The control of the guns was good & NCOs + Team commanders have learned valuable lessons from previous operations in this respect; namely keeping in touch with their Section Officers.

APPENDIX III B

Copy of Final Report on OPERATIONS 23rd Oct.
Sent to No 12 Inf Brigade.
                    By
                    Lieut. W. W. ROBERTON
                    Comd'g No 12 Machine Gun Company.

1. ORDERS Category (a) Bde GR 263 (See Sub Appendix)

    (i) Ref Bde Warning Orders 21st inst
                    Para 6 MACHINE GUNS
        The previous Company Orders issued for
        Operations of 12th and 18th inst & Special Orders
        for Indirect Barrage fire were practically Similar.

    (ii) SPECIAL ORDERS for Indirect Fire Guns
        1. Guns will open fire at ZERO on the
           line N.35.d.5.5 to N.35.a.8.8. till ZERO + 8 min.
        2. At ZERO + 8 min guns will cease fire &
           elevate to 2,500 yds — except centre
           gun firing at CEMETERY — Circle Sunken Rd.
        3. After guns have relayed they will
           open fire again & continue firing till
           ZERO + 35 min when they will at once
           cease fire.
        4. They will then remain in position and
           await further orders.

    Special Notes
        a Section Officers superintending will
           arrange system of control by
           whistle enabling No 1's to know when
           to open or cease fire.
        b The number of rounds fired must
           be noted & reported to O.C. Coy
        c All stoppages must be reported on
        d During & immediately after firing
           steps must be taken to immediately
           refill empty belts.
        e Word must be immediately sent
           back to T.8. Central (H.Q.) asking for
           S.A.A. should it be required, when

III B

Carriers from H.Q. will draw from Bde Dump
& carry up to Advanced Dump.

f. You will establish a Section Dump for S.A.A near
positions, where your carriers & any spare men will
remain

g. Carriers will be utilised to assist in Belt
filling by opening S.A.A boxes & handing out
rounds to Spare gunners.

h. Endeavours should be made to find out
from infantry what was apparent effect
of Indirect Fire, whether bullets cleared their
heads well etc:—

i. It is particularly urgent that reports re
situation be periodically sent back by
runners to H.Q. T.S. Central.

2. Communication:—

a) Runners:—
The following Relay System
of Runners was established for these
Operations.

No 1 Post:— 2 Orderlies with H.Q. 'B' Section.

No 2 Post:— 2 .... 'A' Section.
Special mission Indirect Fire guns
WINDMILL LANE.

No 3 Post (No 3 Bde Post):— T 2 d E 4.
2 orderlies.

No 4 Post:— 2 orderlies at Coy H.Q. T.S.Central.

b) Telephone:—
Telephone Communication was
established with by H.Q. T.S.Central &
No 2 Bde Post in FLEET LINE

The Section in the line received orders
to be in telephone communication with Coy H.Q.
through Bn H.Q. in SUNKEN Rd.

III B

3. <u>Dispositions & Assembly Positions.</u>

For these operations I disposed of
the Company as follows:-

(i) B Section under 2/Lt Lightbody & 2/Lt Grainger.
    <u>a</u> ½ B Section under Sgt Clanner in SPECTRUM
        for enfilading 1st Objective.
    <u>b</u> other ½ B Section under 2/Lt Grainger behind
        THISTLE Tr ready to go forward &
        take up positions in DEWDROP when
        captured.

(ii) SPECIAL MISSION :— Indirect Fire Barrage Guns
        A Section under Lt Bradbury
        ½ C   —   —   Lt Leash.

Indirect fire positions on high ground behind
SUNKEN RD in and near WINDMILL LANE.

(iii) D & other ½ C Section in Reserve in
FLERS LINE near Coy. H Q T.8. Central.

4.   <u>OPERATIONS</u>
    Category (c) Bde GR 963 (see SUB-APPENDIX)
    <u>Action of 'B' Section and Special Mission Guns</u>

For actual report on operations
of above Sections I refer you to my
REPORT ON OPERATIONS 23rd inst :—

APPENDIX IV

Remarks, Criticisms and Suggestions
(Category (e) Bde GR263 (See Sub-Appendix)
By Lieut. W.E. Roberton
Comdg No 12 Machine Gun Company

1. **INDIRECT FIRE:—**

    (a) The barrage fire by the Special Mission Indirect fire guns appeared to be good from the information obtained from the infantry.

    (b) Improved emplacements producing better results could have been erected had there been more time at our disposal:— Machine guns require for continuous prolonged Indirect fire a steady platform.

    (c) Before opening up a large volume of fire I would suggest that each gun fires off a few rounds to warm up the guns, thus ensuring that every gun opens fire at ZERO Hour & preventing to a large extent MINOR STOPPAGES.

2. **CO-OPERATION with INFANTRY**

    It is most important that detail and continuous information be received by Machine Gun Section officers as to the Tactical Situation and Progress of Infantry.
    It is impossible to ensure efficient co-operation unless we receive full information from the infantry.

A.P. IV

2

3. MOBILITY

Owing to its weight a Machine Gun & Mounting should not be hurriedly sent forward to Objective especially when the position is obscure.

In my opinion this was the cause of the confusion and lack of control as regards Action of 'A' Section in Operations 13th Oct
see Page 6 Para D

4. Category (c) Bde G R 263 (See Sub-Appendix)

Equipment and method of carrying

A rifle greatly impairs the carrying power of a Machine Gun Team. At present only Nos 1 & 2 are armed with revolvers, and I think it would be much better if all Machine gunners were armed with revolvers in place of Rifles.

5. Communication

My own Relay System of Runners for Operations 18th and 23rd inst proved quite satisfactory.

W.E. Robertson Lieut.
Comdg No 12 Machine Gun Coy
1-11-10

12th Brigade.

4th Division.

12th INFANTRY BRIGADE

MACHINE GUN COMPANY

NOVEMBER 1916

WAR DIARY or INTELLIGENCE SUMMARY

Army Form C. 2118

Place	Date	Hour	Summary of Events and Information	Remarks and references to Appendices
WOIREL	1/11/16		Uneventful: — Received orders for probable move 3rd inst.	WBR / My Maps. (1) ROSEVILLE Sheet 1/100,000 (2) DIEPPE Sheet 1/100,000 WBR
	2/11/16		Uneventful.	WBR
	3/11/16		Left WOIREL at 9.15 A.M for LE PLOUY — Arrived at our billets 12.30 P.M. — Company H.Q at "OZENE FARM". Company Training: — Received details reinforcement of 2 horses (L.D) + 1 limber G.S Wagon.	WBR
LE PLOUY	4th		Company Billets visited by Divisional Commander.	WBR
	5th		Uneventful: usual Company training.	WBR
	6th		Training: — Received R.B de Route March 2 & 6th inst. — 100 reinforcement.	WBR
	7th		Company and Transport (4 Section limbers) formed up and marched off at 8.30 A.M.	WBR
	8th	8.15 A.M	Route: — VISMES — au — val to Starting Point junction of Road South East of MORVAL — the road junction N of LE TRANSLAY village — Cross Roads E of MARTAINNEVILLE chateau — N of MARTAINNEVILLE Station to ground 500 yds Brigade then formed up and was inspected by Corps and Divisional Commanders.	

WAR DIARY or INTELLIGENCE SUMMARY

Army Form C. 2118

Place	Date	Hour	Summary of Events and Information	Remarks and references to Appendices
LE PLOY	Nov 1915 6th		After inspection NCO's and Men who had received rewards in recent operations were presented with their Medal Ribbons by the Commander.	WER
	9th		Uneventful :— Range Practice	WER
	10th		Range Practice :— 2/Lt E. ROGERS 1 3.O.R. leave to U.K.	WER
	11th		Arrival of CAPT. T. B. BAGER to command Company.	WER
	12th		Parade Church Service :— 1.O.R. returned off leave.	WER
	13th		Uneventful.	WER
	14th		Usual Training.	WER
	15th 9.15AM		Received 12th Bde Training Order No 4 for Brigade Route March. Company and Transport lined up for Brigade Route March and marched off at 9-30 A.M: Passed Starting Point "Cross Rds East of MARTAINNE-VILLE Chateau at 10-42 A.M." Route :— TRANSLAY — HINFRAY — G in MAIGNEVILLE — Cross Roads No 6 of MAIGNEVILLE Village — to Billets." Fell out on March :— Nil. Arrived back in billets about 1-30 P.M.	Ref Map 1/100,000 ABBEVILLE 14 DIEPPE 16.
			2/Lieuts. W. GRAINGER and E.H. ROSE to 4th Div School of Instruction. 2/Lieut. R.M. STRAIGHT Y 3.O.R to leave to U.K.	WER

WAR DIARY or INTELLIGENCE SUMMARY

Army Form C. 2118

Confidential

(Erase heading not required.)

Place	Date Nov 16	Hour	Summary of Events and Information	Remarks and references to Appendices
LE PLOUY	16th		Usual Company Training: — Leave Cancelled.	WER
	17th		2/Lieut. STRAIGHT & 3 O.R. rejoined owing to leave being cancelled.	WER
	18th		Company paid out in the afternoon 2-45 P.M:	WER
	19th		2/Lieut. T.E. HAMMOND rejoined from course at School of Transport HAVRE: — Usual Church Service.	WER
	20th		2/Lieut. R.M. STRAIGHT and 3 O.R. leave to U.K. 2/Lieut. J. LIGHTBODY rejoined from leave to U.K. "A" Company 2/Lancs Fusiliers at football at MAISNEVILLE Company team played — Company won 2 – 1.	WER
	21st		Usual Company Training. — 3 O.R. to U.K. leave.	WER
	22nd		C.S.M. & 1 N.C.O. to Div Anti-gas School for a course.	WER
	23rd		2/Lieut. ROGERS & 1 O.R. rejoined from leave U.K.	WER
	24th		G.O.C. Brigade paid a visit to the Company about 12-45 P.M. Company also [informed?] by D.V. Jockin at [?] MESNIL Visits to Company by Lt Col CLARKE X.V. Corps M.G.O. 10R rejoined from leave Lt WEROBERTON to 3 OR proceed on leave to MG Corps at CAMIERS. 1 OR to 4th Army Coping School	WER
	25th		Lt E ROGERS + 2 OR to MG [Corps?] at CAMIERS.	
	26th		Lt J LIGHTBODY to [?] GRANTHAM	
	27th		Company [?] Won 2–1.	
	28th		Company firing 11 [?] MG Coy. [?] Wounds [?]	
	29th			
	30th			

[signature] Major
Commanding No. 12[?] Coy

12th Brigade.

4th Division.

========

12th INFANTRY BRIGADE

MACHINE GUN COMPANY

DECEMBER 1916

SECRET.

WAR. DIARY.
OF
12TH MACHINE GUN COMPANY.

Vol 12

FROM 1st December 1916   To 31st December 1916

(VOLUME 12)

Army Form C. 2118.

WAR DIARY
or
INTELLIGENCE SUMMARY.
(Erase heading not required.)

Instructions regarding War Diaries and Intelligence
Summaries are contained in F. S. Regs., Part II.
and the Staff Manual respectively. Title pages
will be prepared in manuscript.

Place	Date	Hour	Summary of Events and Information	Remarks and references to Appendices
LE PLOUY	Dec/1916 1st	1-30 P.M.	The Transport left LE PLOUY at 1-30 P.M. — destination WOIREL arrived there 5-0 P.M. The Company carried out drill in the morning & football in the afternoon at LE PLOUY.	WBR
LE PLOUY	2nd		The Transport left WOIREL for LONGPRÉ – AMIENS at 6-30 A.M. – billeted Serres to water Feed. — The Company (less transport) remained during day at LE PLOUY	WBR
	3rd	2-0 A.M.	Reveille, and shortly after the hour the Company (less transport) fell in to march off to entraining station OISEMONT. — Company entrained at 12 NOON and detrained at MERICOURT – L'ABBÉ.	Ref Map Sheet ALBERT 1/40,000 WBR
CAMP 107 N.E. of BRAY-SUR-SOMME			BRAY-SUR-SOMME, arriving there about 6-30 P.M. It then marched to CAMP 107. N.E. of	
	4th	10-0 A.M.	was arrived at same Camp at 6-0 P.M. The Transport The Company & transport left Camp 107 at 10-0 A.M. – destination Camp in BILLON WOOD East of BRONFAY FARM & arrived there at 2-0 P.M.	WBR
CAMP E. of BRONFAY FM.	5th		Company remained all day in camp cleaning & refitting arms — received 12th Brigade Operation Order No 56 about the coming relief: – Capt BIB & 2/Lt COHEN proceeded to the H.Q.s of ?	WBR
MARICOURT CAMP (A.II.b.d.3.3)	6th	10-30 A.M.	At 10-30 A.M. The Company & Transport marched off to MARICOURT Camp near A.II.b.d.3.3) ? — Capt BABB & 2/Lt COHEN rejoined Company. — 3.O.R. proceeded on leave to U.K. & arrived there about 12-15 P.M.	WBR

2353 Wt. W2544/1454 700,000 5/15 D. D. & L. A.D.S.S./Forms/C. 2118.

WAR DIARY or INTELLIGENCE SUMMARY

Army Form C. 2118.

Place	Date Dec 1916	Hour	Summary of Events and Information	Remarks and references to Appendices
Trenches	7th	10.0A.M.	2/Lt COMEFFY + H.Q. Party proceeded to take over positions from the FRENCH 20th Corps — at 2-0 P.M. C.S.M. WARD + remainder of H.Q. proceeded to take over Company H.Q. in the line near Bde H.Q. at MOUCHOIR COPSE (T.24.b.5.9). — 'D' + 'C' Section also left the camp at 2-0 P.M.:- destination, 'D' Section a cellar in COMBLES, and ½ C Section CROSS RDS at (U.20.A.1.9) to take up positions in Bde Support Line, other ½ C Section in FREGICOURT line	See APPENDIX 8 copy of 1-2 Bde OO No 56 mls WSR Col of line COMBLES 7.5m 20,000
"		7.0 P.M.	A+B Sections proceeded with the Commanding Officer to take over positions in the Front + Support Lines as follows. — 'A' Section took over + front line positions in Left Bde Sector + 2 guns of 'B' Section in Right Bde Sector — 'B' Section took over 2 positions in ½ C Section at X RDS. — the remaining 2 teams of B Section took up positions with ½ C Section at X RDS. — The transport moved off to new lines with O.M.S. Stores + settled with rest of 1st line transport of Bde near (B.13.a.1.4.) West of MAUREPAS.	WSR
"	8th	8.0	the night of 7/8th Dec the relief of 10 positions in the line proceeded satisfactorily + the relief was reported complete early morning of the 8th. — 8 O.R. off from each Battalion were attached to the Company as drivers — 10. O.R. rejoined the Company transport from leave U.K.	WSR

WAR DIARY
INTELLIGENCE SUMMARY

Army Form C. 2118.

Place	Date	Hour	Summary of Events and Information	Remarks and references to Appendices
Trenches	9th Dec 1916		Situation Normal during the day: — 3.O.R. rejoined Company from leave U.K.	W.E.R.
"	10th		Bde Relief orders received: — 2 O.R. attached Carriers slightly wounded by a shell near Coy. H.Q.: — rest of the day uneventful.	W.E.R.
"	11th		Coy. H.Q. shelled during the day & night: — Inter Section Relief, viz: "A" Section from Front line to COMBLES, "D" Section from COMBLES to Fontaine road leading up to Company Dump. "B" & "C" Sections changed over.	W.E.R.
"	12th		shelled, delaying Transport: — received 1st Bde GR 41 "Works required addenda & Corr: Slip" H.Q. again slightly shelled, otherwise uneventful. — 1.O.R. rejoined from leave U.K.: — 2/Lt GRAINGER & ROSE rejoined from 4th Div School.	W.E.R.
"	13th		Lt ROBERTON rejoined from Leave U.K.: — 2.O.R. proceeded on leave U.K. — 1.O.R. reinforcement joined Company: — Anti Aircraft position at	W.E.R.
"	14th		(T.2.B.D.8.7.) was occupied by 2 teams "A" Section from COMBLES. Received 12th Bde. O.O. No 59 re relief of battalions night of 15/16th inst:— day quite normal: — work carried on enlarging H.Q. dug-out.	W.E.R. mah Ref Sheet 57C.S.W. (57 B 1.25 2/5000) W.E.R.

Place	Date	Hour	Summary of Events and Information	Remarks and references to Appendices
Trenches	15th Oct 1916		3.O.T. proceeded on leave U.K. :— day normal :— during the evening's night 15/16th inst inter-battalion relief, & the following inter-section Relief;- 'C' Section relieved 'A' Section. - 2 Teams at COMBLES + 2 Teams at Anti-Aircraft Position. 'A' Section took over positions, 2 teams Right Front line + 2 teams at BULLET X RDS / previously occupied by 'C' Section :— 'B' Section relieved 'D' Section of H Front Line Positions, after relief 'D' Section took over positions at X RDS + Positions Reserve near H.Q FREICOURT Line: — After the relief the disposition of the Company was as follows :— A Section :- { 2 Teams Front Line Right Sector. { 2 Teams at BULLET X RDS. B Section :- 4 teams in Front Line Left Sector. C Section :- { 2 Teams in COMBLES. { 2 Teams at Anti-Aircraft Position D Section :- { 2 Teams Reserve FREICOURT Line { 2 Teams BULLET X RDS. This relief was reported complete at 6-45 P.M. evening 15th Inst.	WSR WSR

WAR DIARY
INTELLIGENCE SUMMARY

Army Form C. 2118.

Place	Date Dec 1916	Hour	Summary of Events and Information	Remarks and references to Appendices
Trenches	16th		Lieut. E. ROGERS & 2.O.R rejoined from Machine Gun Course CAMIERS. Lt.Col. CLARKE, Machine Gun Officer XV Corps visited Coy. H.Q & the line. Received 4th Div. No. 9307 "4th Div. Billeting List in Forward Area".	
"	17th		Uneventful :- Continuation of work on Coy. H.Q.	WER
"	18th		Situation quiet + uneventful. — Received 12th Bde O.O. No. 60 re 4th Battalion relief night of 19/20th inst. — Lt. BRADBURY & 2.O.R rejoined from leave.	WER
"	19th		Inter-Section Relief :- C Section relieved B Section in Front Line left sector on the evening of the 19th inst.	WER
"	20th		Normal :- "Received Defence Scheme of left sectors of 4th Division Front." 2.O.R proceeded on leave U.K. — Received 12th Bde. O.O. No. 61 re relief of the Brigade by the 10th Bde on the night of 23/24th inst. Company Relief Orders for 23rd inst issued.	See APPENDIX B
"	21st		Situation quiet :- Uneventful.	
"	22nd		Normal :- — 2 Officers of 10th M.G. Company visited H.Q. re relief. Major Low, O.C. 10th M.G. Company paid a visit to Company & reconnoitred the line.	
"	23rd		Received 4th Div. G.G.67/4 re detachment T I Sector from Company for Anti-Aircraft duties with IV Army Anti-Aircraft Group round COMBLES - MAUREPAS & LE FOREST areas. — A letter from the Company to	WER

WAR DIARY
or
INTELLIGENCE SUMMARY.
(Erase heading not required.)

Army Form C. 2118.

Place	Date Dec 1916	Hour	Summary of Events and Information	Remarks and references to Appendices
Trenches	22nd		To relieve a section of 40th Div on the 27th inst :-	WER
"	23rd		During the morning the Transport & Q.M.S stores moved to Camp 16 :- Received Amended instructions re attd to WDiv G.G.S 67/4. "Anti-Aircraft gns" :-	See APPENDIX B
		4.30 PM	Guides met 10th Machine Gun Company & relief proceeded :- Relief reported complete about 11 P.M. :- after relief Section proceeded independently in Motor Lorries to Camp 16 (F.30.a.9.1.) :- all Company reported same arrived in camp at 1.0 A.M. 24th inst.	Part of Relieving Relief.
"	24th	1.0 AM	All Company arrived at Camp 16 :- Spent the day resting :-	WER
		2. O.R	rejoined from leave – D. HAMMOND & 2.O.R. proceed on leave to U.K.	WER
"	25th		Church parade Service for all denominations at 11.0 A.M. :- Received 12th Bn. GR No 88/2 re amended instructions Anti-Aircraft Section.	WER
"	26th		Uneventful :- Lt BRADBURY & 2 teams of C Section proceeded to Road June B.15.a.7.7. to meet an officer of 120th Bde M.G. Coy from there was taken to anti-aircraft position, relieving 2 teams 120th M.G. Coy in accordance with instructions in WDiv G.G.S 67/4 re relief of 4th Div in the line by the 8th Division. Received 12th Inf Brigade O.O. No 62	WER

WAR DIARY
INTELLIGENCE SUMMARY

Army Form C. 2118

Place	Date	Hour	Summary of Events and Information	Remarks and references to Appendices
Camp 16 (F.30.A.9.1)	27th		2/Lt COMERY admitted to hospital; Received Amendment (No1) to 12th Bde.O.O. 62 and March Table:—	WER
"	28th	10.0A.M.	Company orders to move issued. Company transport laid up near starting point BRONFAY farm transport delayed in starting. — Company proceeding without transport at 10.5 A.M.	
		1.15 P.M.	Company arrived at destination SAILLY-LAURETTE, met billeting party 2/Lt GRAINGER & 3.O.R. who had proceeded earlier in advance; Coy H.Q. were established at No 12 billet. — Transport arrived about 1 hour later.	WER
SAILLY-LAURETTE	29th		Uneventful.	WER
"	30th		Uneventful.	
"	31st		Usual Church Parade Services: ——— Lt. LEAST, C.S.M. WARD & 1.O.R. leave for U.K.	WER

APPENDIX A (1)

Ref. Sheet ALBERT. 1/40,000.

Copy of **12th Infantry Brigade Operation Order No. 56**

5/12/16.

1. The 4th Division will relieve a portion of the French 20th Corps on the front approximately between V.20.b.5.5. and the Sunken Road (inclusive north of SAILLISEL at V.14.b.6.4.

2. The 10th Infantry Brigade will be on the right and will take over part of the section held by the French 11th Division, and the 12th Infantry Brigade will be on the left and will take over part of the line held by the French 39th Division.

3. The 12th Infantry Brigade will take over the Southern part of the Front held by the French 78th Brigade on the evening of the 7th inst. The 10th Infantry Brigade will take over their line on the evening of the 8th inst.

4. Movements to the line will be carried out according to the attached Move Table.
   All details of relief will be arranged between OCs Units concerned.

5. The Brigade will be disposed in the line as follows:-

Right Front Battalion	Duke of Wellingtons.
Left Front Battalion	King's Own.
Close support Battalion	Lan. Fus.
Reserve Battalion (FREGICOURT.)	Essex.
Machine Gun Company	4 Guns in Bn support line
	4 Guns in Bde support line (BERLIN TR. Area)
	4 Guns in FREGICOURT line
	4 Guns in Reserve near COMBLES.
T.M. Battery	In reserve Temporarily at MAUREPAS Camp (B.13.b.7.4) near FREGICOURT.
1/1st. Renfrew Field Coy R.E.	
Brigade Headquarters	MOUCHOIR Copse (T.24.b.5.9.)

- Brigade Report Centre   U.19.b.8.8.
  R.E. Dump.   U.19.a.2.4.
  1st line Transport and   West of MAUREPAS. near
  Qr. MR's Stores   B.13.a.1.4.

6. The following places are in view of the enemy:-
   (a) All ground East of the Main SAILLY-SAILLISEL — RANCOURT. Road.
   (b) The ground about T.24. Central to road West of that point.
   (c) Ground between T.24. Central and V.15. Central Except in case of an attack or in a fog, this ground will not be crossed in daylight except by parties of not greater number than 3.

7. <u>Traffic</u> Rations and stores will not pass East of MAUREPAS until after dark. Single vehicles if urgently required may move in daylight to FREGICOURT. Church using the road through T.29.a. (COMBLES)

8. <u>Artillery</u> The French artillery will not be relieved until the 11th inst.

9. <u>Communication</u> Telephone lines are laid to Battalion H.Q. from Brigade H.Q.

10. Routes during relief will be:-
    (a) To the Front:-
        By MARICOURT. – HARBICOURT. – MAUREPAS. Rd
    (b) From the Front
        By MAUREPAS. – FERME ROUGE Road.

11. Instructions for taking over the line:-
    The dispositions of Companies and Battalions will be the same as held by the French.
    Lewis Guns will relieve Machine Guns of the French in the front line,

and Vickers Guns those in the support line.

A French Officer will remain for 24 hours after relief, with each British Unit

12. There is water for water carts and horses at MAUREPAS HALTE.

13. Completion of relief will be reported to Brigade Headquarters when the G.O.C. 12th Infantry Brigade will assume Command of the line.

APPENDIX B

(1)

Copy of
Relief Orders
By
Captain J.B. BABER. M.C.
Commanding 12th Machine Gun Company

1. The Company will be relieved by the 10th Machine Gun Company on the night 23rd/24th inst

11. After relief the Company will move in buses to Camp 16. and will be in Divisional Reserve.

Details of Relief

1. Guides:- O.C. Sections concerned will detail the following guides to meet the incoming Gun Teams of the 10th Company.
   a. 1 Guide for H.Q.
   b. 1 " " H.Q. Sub Section Artillery dug-out
   c. 1 " " Anti-Aircraft positions
   d. 2 Guides for CROSS Roads positions
   e. 6 Guides for FRONT line positions

Meeting Point for above guides :- end of C.T. on FREGICOURT. Road. guides to be at this point at 6-0 P.M. 23rd inst.

O.C. 'B' Section will detail 1 guide to meet incoming ½ Section to COMBLES at CEMETERY Cross Roads 5-30 P.M. 23rd inst

Section Officers will provide each guide with a slip of paper having the name of the positions marked on it

The 12th Machine Gun Company will hand over to 10th Machine Gun Company 6 Belt boxes per gun for following positions

6 guns in front line - 36 Boxes ⎫ Total
4 guns at X Roads - 24 " ⎬ 60 Boxes

- O.C.'s 'C', and 'D' Sections will obtain signed receipts for all Belt Boxes handed over to 10th Company which concerns them

3. All trench stores and any trench maps will be handed over and receipts obtained. A syllabus of work proposed and work in hand will also be given to incoming Sections. NO Gum boots will be handed over, but will be taken out by Sections and loaded on transport

4. All signed receipts from handing over will be forwarded to Company Office at Camp 16. on arrival.

5. Lieut H. BRADBURY. and 1 man per team from 6 front line positions will remain behind in the line with 10th Company until evening of 24th to assist them

6. TRANSPORT. arrangements.
   a. 1 limber for 2 teams 'B' Section at COMBLES to be at CEMETERY. X Roads 6-0 P.M. on 23rd inst
   b. 1 limber for 2 teams 'B' Section at Anti Aircraft position at 6-0 P.M.
   c. 2 limbers for 2 teams 'A' Section (artillery dug-outs) and H.Q. at 6-0 P.M.
   d. 1 limber for 4 teams Cross Rds at 7-15. P.M.
   e. 2 limbers for 6 front line teams at 8-0 P.M.

NOTE :- With the exception of ½ Section in COMBLES the Transport will come up to the usual dump - viz bottom of C.T. entrance to FREGICOURT. at the times stated above for each Section

7. 2 Lieut W.J.H. GRAINGER. will report completion of relief of front line guns at Coy H.Q. on his way back from the line

8. After relief Sections will march off independantly to Assembly Point - viz 200 yards south of Road junction B.14..a.9.3. (west of MAUREPAS) Here Buses will be waiting to convey Company to Camp 16

(3)

9. After loading up limbers will move off independently to Transport lines

10. Section Officers will detail 1 Brakesman per limber to accompany transport

11. <u>Advance party</u>:- 2 Lieut F. COMERY. 1 Company cook at COMBLES, 1 man from 'A' Section and 1 man from 'B' Section will proceed as an advance party to Camp 16. and take over 10th Company Billets

They will leave early morning 23rd inst. Cooks cart will accompany them to the camp to enable Hot tea to be prepared and ready for arrival of Company early 24th inst

Acknowledge.

21/12/16

W E Roberton Lieut
Adjt 12th Machine Gun Company

4th Division

12th Infantry Bde

12th M. G. C.

January, To December
1917.

Vol/13

CONFIDENTIAL

WAR DIARY

OF

12TH Machine Gun Company

From 1st January 1917 To 31st January 1917

(VOLUME 13.)

Army Form C. 2118.

WAR DIARY
or
INTELLIGENCE SUMMARY.
(Erase heading not required.)

Place	Date	Hour	Summary of Events and Information	Remarks and references to Appendices
SAILLY-LAURETTE	Jan 1	morn	O.C. visited Coy at Coy training. 8 O.R. rejoined from leave	gm
		noon	Football	gm
		2pm 4pm	Company training. 1 O.R. from leave. 1 O.R. to Hospital	gm
	3	m	Capt Anderson visits Coy at Coy training. 2 Reinforcements from Rein Bns. Football. Coy training.	gm
	4	a/m p/m	4 O.R. joined on leave	gm
	5	— 4pm	Notification received of Lieut Robertson to proceed to 25th Coy to command + Lieut morris to join vice Robertson. Football	gm
	6		4 O.R. proceed on leave	gm

Army Form C. 2118.

WAR DIARY
or
INTELLIGENCE SUMMARY.
(Erase heading not required.)

Instructions regarding War Diaries and Intelligence Summaries are contained in F. S. Regs., Part II. and the Staff Manual respectively. Title pages will be prepared in manuscript.

Place	Date	Hour	Summary of Events and Information	Remarks and references to Appendices
SALLY-LAURETTE	Jan 7		Dis Xmas day. Concert in evening	
	8	6pm-10pm	Coy training	
	9	pm	Coy training	
		am	Football	
	10	am+pm	Coy training. 1 O/R reinforcement from Base Depot. Joint Harness from leave	
	11	am	Coy training	
		pm	Football. 2 Lieut Farmyer & Lieut Croston return to Bradbury & remainder at Alanupon at LE FORET	
	12	am+pm	Coy training. 1 OR reported from leave	

2353 Wt. W-3544/1454 700,000 5/15 D. D. & L. A.D.S.S./Forms/C. 2118.

WAR DIARY
or
INTELLIGENCE SUMMARY.

(Erase heading not required.)

Army Form C. 2118.

Place	Date	Hour	Summary of Events and Information	Remarks and references to Appendices
SAILLY		m	Coy Training	P.M
LAURETTE	Jan 13	a/n	Football	
			WOR proceed on leave	
		10 midn	Coy training	P.M
			9th Lovat's discharged from hospital	
			2 OR to M.G. school. 4th Rifles then proceed on account of illness	
			1 OR contracts German Measles	
		15 m	Coy Training	P.M
		a/n	Football	
			Lt Hammond & 2 OR to 4 Div school	
			Lt Bradbury proceed to M.G. school	
			Remainder of B Coy relieves 2 lines along aircraft at LE FORET	P.M
			B codn. rendered on account of German aircraft (11 can) bullet dropfire	

Army Form C. 2118.

WAR DIARY
or
INTELLIGENCE SUMMARY.
(Erase heading not required.)

Instructions regarding War Diaries and Intelligence Summaries are contained in F. S. Regs., Part II. and the Staff Manual respectively. Title pages will be prepared in manuscript.

Place	Date	Hour	Summary of Events and Information	Remarks and references to Appendices
SAILLY LAURETTE	16	morning	Coy Training & Baths.	P.m.
	17	"	Coy Training. C.S.M. & 2 O/r return from leave; 2 o/r from W Brest hotel then Xmas dinner	a.m. p.m.
	18	"	Coy Training	p.m.
	19	"	Coy Training	p.m.
	20	"	Coy Training	p.m.
	21	"	Coy Training	p.m.
	22	"	Coy Training; Orders for move to new area received; Operation order No 1 issued	a.m. p.m.

2 & 6.15 FORÊT DOMANIAL shot down a hostile aeroplane with 3 M.Gs in team. Coy claims 1 gun as trophy.

WAR DIARY
or
INTELLIGENCE SUMMARY

Army Form C. 2118.

Place	Date	Hour	Summary of Events and Information	Remarks and references to Appendices
S. LAURETTE	23		Coy moves to BRAY. 1 lorry allotted + 1 G.S. wagon lent by No 4 Coy A.S.C. Billets at BRAY v. poor. Coy operations news no 2 coowrd	
BRAY	24		Coy moves to SUZANNE. Billeted in 1 hut + a few spare sheds very crowded	
SUZANNE	25		Two guns detailed for A. Aircraft duty. 2 mile from billets. Guns remain to ready phone. no aeroplane shot down.	
	26		Coy training	
	27		Coy training. C.O. Reconnoitres the line.	
	28		Sunday Church Service. Heut P. Morgan & 2/Lt G.C. Berry join for duty. Lieut Keath reports from sick leave in U.K.	
	29		Coy Training. O'Mason posted to D. Tr. Lt Berry & 2/Lt G.C. Berry reconnoitre line held by 11 M.G. Coy.	

Army Form C. 2118.

WAR DIARY
or
INTELLIGENCE SUMMARY.

(Erase heading not required.)

Place	Date	Hour	Summary of Events and Information	Remarks and references to Appendices
SUZANNE	30		Coy training. 2/Lt Mason & 2/Lt Leask reconnoitre gun positions in front line. 2.0. & Lt Emery attend Corps lecture on a/aircraft English [?] M.G.s. "Antiaircraft Instructions" issued to Pn Offrs.* Coy operation orders No 3 issued.	*Appendix
	31	am	G.O.C. 4th Div presents M.M. ribbon to C.Q.M.S. Roberts, 2 offrs & 30 men from Coy attend parade. Coy hold lot 23" Div order.	

SECRET.   Copy No 3

No 12 Machine Gun Company OPERATION ORDER No 1.

Jan 22nd 1917

1. **Parade** :- Company will parade in Transport Yard at 9-20 A.M. on 23rd inst and will move off to new area in following Order., H.Q., 'A', 'B', 'C', and 'D' Sections followed by transport

2. **Packing of limbers** :- All available stores will be packed in limbers by 4-30 P.M. 22nd inst. Packing will be finished by 8-30 A.M. 23rd inst. Packs will be carried on limbers

3. **Billeting Party** :- Coy Qr Mr Sgt Roberts and Sgt Corless will leave at 7-30 A.M. as billeting party and will report to Town Major. Camp 112 before 10-30 A.M.

4. **Cooks** :- One limber will leave at 7-30 AM with Company cooks who will prepare dinner for the Company on arrival.

5. **Allotment of limbers** :- Limbers will be alloted as follows :-
'A', 'B', and 'D' Sections   2 limbers each (Blankets on Officers Mess and 'C' Section 2 limbers   SAA limber)
blankets of 'C' section on limber with Officers mess
Cooks and ½ Qr Mr Stores   1 limber
Remainder Qr Mr Stores   1 "
S.A.A.   3 "

Lieut
A/Adjt 12th Machine Gun Company

Issued at 11-45 A.M.
Copy No. 1.   Officers Mess
  "   " 2.   Coy Sgt Mjr for File
  "   " 3.   War Diary

SECRET.   Copy No 3

No Machine Gun Company Operation Order No 2.

23rd Jan 17

1. <u>Parade</u> :- The Company will move into New Billets at SUZANNE on 24th inst. parading in front of Transport billet at 11-20 A.M.

2. <u>Billeting Party</u> :- A billeting party composed of 2nd Lieut F. COMERY, Coy. Qr Mr Sgt ROBERTS and Sgt CORLESS, will leave at 9-0 AM and report to Town Commandant SUZANNE by 10-0 AM 24th inst.

3. <u>Cooks</u> :- Cooks cart will leave at 9-30 AM with Company Cooks as on 23rd inst to prepare dinner for Company.

4. <u>Blankets and Valises</u> :- Officers Valises will be packed, and blankets will be rolled (and inspected by Section Commanders) by 8-30 A.M., ready to be loaded on lorry

5. <u>Packing Limbers</u> :- All wagons will be packed by 10-30 A.M.

Lieut
A/Adjt 12th Machine Gun Company

Issued at 4-30 P.M.
Copy No 1. Officers Mess.
"   " 2 Coy Sgt Mjr for File
"   " 3 War Diary

SECRET.   Copy No 3

Amendment to No 12 Machine Gun Company Operation Order No 2.

                                              23rd Jan 1917

1. <u>For Paragraph 1. Read</u>:- Parading at 2-20 P.M.

2. <u>For Paragraph 2. Read</u>:- Will leave at 12-15 P.M. and report to Town Commandant SUZANNE by 1-0 P.M. 24th inst

3. <u>For Paragraph 3. Read</u>:- Cooks cart will leave at 12-30 P.M.

                                              <u>Lieut.</u>
                                  <u>A/Adjt- No 12 Machine Gun Company</u>

Issued at 9-30 P.M.
Copy No. 1. Officers Mess
  "   " 2, Coy Sgt Mjr for File
  "   " 3, War Diary

SECRET.   Copy No 3.

No 12. Machine Gun Company Operation Order No 3
                                                    30th Jan 1917

1. No 12. Machine Gun Company will relieve No 11. Machine Gun Company in the line on the night 1st/2nd February 1917.

2. Disposition of Sections will be:-

   1. In Front Line
      Left Sector 'D' Section
      Right Sector 'B' Section

   2. In Intermediate Line
      Left Sector 'C' Section
      Right Sector 'A' Section

3. Company will parade at 2-15 P.M. on the 1st prox outside Company Hut. Dress, Fighting Order, Overcoats will be worn. Packs will be left in Fighting limbers under charge of limber Corporal, and will not be taken into the trenches.

4. The Cooks cart and water cart under charge of Coy Qr Mr Sgt will leave at 1-0 P.M. and proceed in advance to CURLU where the Coy Qr Mr Sgt will select a suitable spot for the Company to halt and tea will be issued on arrival of the Company at 4-30 P.M.

5. Each Section will leave 32 filled belt boxes in the Qr Mr Stores, and take only 16 Boxes into the trenches with them.

6. After passing CURLU, 100 yds will be kept between Sections.

7. Limbers will accompany Sections as far as JUNCTION WOOD where Sections will be met at 6-0 P.M. by 1 guide per Section who will lead them to Coy HQ at MARRIERES WOOD where they will meet the guides for each team.
   Spare Part boxes may be left at Coy HQ under care of Coy Sgt Mjr.

8. Water bottles will be filled before parade. 8 Petrol tins will be packed in gun limbers of 'B' and 'D' Sections to be taken into the trenches.

9. Relief will be reported complete without delay, one orderly per Section will be attached to 'B' and 'D' Sections for this purpose.

10. Company transport less gun limbers and HQ limber will move in accordance with separate instructions communicated to Transport Officer.

                                              Hunt
                                    A/Adjt No 12 Machine Gun Company

Issued at 7-45 P.M.
Copy No 1. Officers Mess
"   No 2. Coy Sgt Mjr For File
"   3. War diary

CONFIDENTIAL

WAR DIARY

OF

No 12 MACHINE GUN COMPANY.

FROM 1 February 1917. To 28th February 1917.

(VOLUME. 12.)

Army Form C. 2118.

WAR DIARY
or
INTELLIGENCE SUMMARY.
(Erase heading not required.)

Instructions regarding War Diaries and Intelligence Summaries are contained in F.S. Regs., Part II. and the Staff Manual respectively. Title pages will be prepared in manuscript.

Place	Date	Hour	Summary of Events and Information	Remarks and references to Appendices
SUZANNE	24/1/17	10-0 A.M.	Finish packing limbers and get ready for our journey for against front-line.	P.M.
"	"	2.15 P.M.	Start off for the line to relieve the 11th Company	
CURLU	"	3-30 P.M.	Arrive CURLU and halt for tea. Transport stay here whilst Coy. is in line.	
"	"	5-0 P.M.	Coy. march off accompanied by Lewis gun limbers.	S.M.
JUNCTION WOOD	"	7-30 P.M.	Arrive JUNCTION WOOD at 7-30 P.M. and proceed by communication trench to MARRIERES WOOD where Company H.Q. is to be situated.	
MARRIERES WOOD			Sections arrive at long intervals, and each team picks up its guides for the trenches here. Relief very slow owing to congested trenches.	
"	26/1/17	3-30 A.M.	Relief of 11th Company completed. C.O. and O/Adjt. visit left sector under Lieut. MASON and find them fairly comfortable with good dug-outs and fair emplacements.	S.M.
"	"	7-30 A.M.	C.O., and O/Adjt. return to Coy. H.Q. B.O. and Lieut. F. COMERY go to 112 Camp BRAY. to attend demonstration of Anti-Aircraft firing.	
"	"	9-0 A.M.	Endeavours made to organise the 2n men attached to Coy as Carriers to supply the rations to front line teams. 4 men sent to a dump	

WAR DIARY
or
INTELLIGENCE SUMMARY.

(Erase heading not required.)

Army Form C. 2118.

Place	Date	Hour	Summary of Events and Information	Remarks and references to Appendices
	28/1/17	9.0 AM	about 1½ miles from Bry HQ and these men bring up the rations on the DECAUVILLE light railway. From Bry HQ ration parties take rations and one tin of water per team to front line. Working party under Lieut IONNS is making a mined dug-out in Right sector under Lieut LEASK.	PM
	"	5.0 PM	Received Orders to have a list S.O.S. signal from MARRIERES RIDGE but have not got a Véry light for the rockets, so make rather a mess of it. Two rockets ascend, and two nearly kill no one.	
	Jan 30/17	5-6 AM	Our front heavily bombarded. Raid by enemy anticipated. Shelling dies down about 6-0 AM.	
	"	9-0 AM	Received news that the enemy have entered our trenches on left. One of Lieut MASON's guns is knocked out, and 3 men of Lieut LEASK's section wounded.	
	"	11-0 AM	Brigade Major informs us we have a Boche prisoner left behind by raiding party.	
	"	9.30 PM	C.O. visits guns in intermediate line, no guns have frozen yet although the frost is very keen. All guns are wrapped round with several	

WAR DIARY
or
INTELLIGENCE SUMMARY.
(Erase heading not required.)

Army Form C. 2118.

Place	Date	Hour	Summary of Events and Information	Remarks and references to Appendices
MARRIERES WOOD	2/11/17		thicknesses of newspaper and the whole toured round with a putter the barrel casing is filled with glycerine 1 pint, water 3½ pints, and the oil is mixed with an equal quantity of paraffin. This works very well indeed. When possible a blanket is put over the gun when it is mounted and received shot toroids are fired, and the gun is shaken every ½ to 1 an hour.	
		9-0 pm	C.O. visits all front line guns	pm
			Trench routine continues. Both sections in front system are busy improving emplacements, and preparing the trench for a chain. They are also making 4 mined dug-outs. Each section in intermediate line supply a carrying party to take timber etc to these sections. Our gunners bombard enemy trenches the whole day, individually they bombard our trenches too from LEASK. Much annoyed.	
			C.O visits all gun positions in evening	
			Lieut LEASK dispersing enemy working party in early hours of morning	f(1)
	24/6/17		Pte HARRISON died of wounds received in 3rd inst.	

WAR DIARY
~~INTELLIGENCE SUMMARY~~
(Erase heading not required.)

Army Form C. 2118.

Place	Date	Hour	Summary of Events and Information	Remarks and references to Appendices
MARIERES WOOD	14/7/16		C.O. and 9a/p visit gun positions in Right sector in the evening. Everything O.K. Lieut MASON shoots a sniper.	(M)
"	15/7/16		8" Howitzers bombard hour LEASK and inflict casualties on the Infantry. Ring strafe in the afternoon. 8 guns of 12th Bat. 8-guns of 33rd Division, and 8 guns of 23rd Bde. get into action side by side and put on a flank barrage on the Bosche trenches. C.O. guns two twelve belts indirect, result one broken trench. Larger spring probably due to the cold and one broken muzzle cap. Each gun began near the immediately. Owing to the severe frost this is very satisfactory. Belt filling 96 belts to fill. Lieut GRAINGER takes two to collect empty cases, about 14 Thursday's full. Bosche has "wind up" and keeps sending up lights all night. Working parties dispersed by hints LEASK's and MASON's guns.	(M)
"	16/7/16		Right sector mostly inactive and plans for night firing laid.	(M)

WAR DIARY

or INTELLIGENCE SUMMARY

Army Form C. 2118.

Place	Date	Hour	Summary of Events and Information	Remarks and references to Appendices
MARRIERES WOOD	11/9/17	6 pm	Lieut H. BRADBURY arrives at Bgy H.Q. having lost his servant and mules during journey from CAMIERS.	AM
"	12/9/17		Lieuts LEASK and MASON come to Bgy HQ to reconnoitre intermediate lines in preparation for under decision tonight. Stokes comp to proceed for under relieves at Bgy H.Q. 8 Mine fuses to known dug-outs arranged. Several Aeroplanes engaged but nothing doing. Brigadier General 12 Brigade visits Bgy H.Q. to arrange plans for a stunt. New Brigade Major comes in afternoon.	AM
"	12/9/17		Outbreak for a raid by the Dukes to night 12/13 Machine Gun Company to give flank barrage fire and also create a diversion on the left. 2 OR minnie gunner on the SOMME and one provided by M.M.P.	PM
"	13/9/17		Trench routine continues & Letters of 11/8 Bn come to take part in a big all night shoot. Heavy German barrage	PM

WAR DIARY
or
INTELLIGENCE SUMMARY

Army Form C. 2118

Place	Date	Hour	Summary of Events and Information	Remarks and references to Appendices
	12 Feb 17		Put down over front line when guns open fire. Dukes raid postponed	a.m.
	13 Feb 17		Trench routine continues	
	14 Feb 17		Trench routine continues	
	15 Feb 17		O.C. 112 Company comes up to take over in preparation for to-morrow relief	p.m.
	16 Feb 17		Relieved by 112 Company. March trek to LOITER CAMP with the exception of 'B' & 'D' Sections who remain in for a shoot in conjunction with 112 Company. C.O. goes to MARRIERES WOOD to experience instructions for the Company's part in 8 Division attack on night of 18 Division.	p.m.
	17 Feb 17		A & C Sections go up to line starting from LOITER CAMP at 5 A.M. The Company is at the disposal of 19 Company for 24 hours up to ZERO hour of the 8 Division attack.	
	18 Feb 17		8 Division attack is cancelled. Company comes out of the line to LOITER CAMP last section arriving at 7.30 p.m. One man falls and breaks his wrist.	p.m.
LOITER CAMP	20 Feb 17		Company march to Camp 117 parading at 12.30 p.m. destination at 9.30 a.m. reaches Camp 117 in men fall out very creditable after 18 days in the trenches.	
CAMP 117	21 Feb 17		Company leaves Camp 117 at 10.20 and arrives CORBIE at 1.30 p.m. No men fell out. Company marched very well and had cleaned itself very thoroughly.	

WAR DIARY
or
INTELLIGENCE SUMMARY

(Erase heading not required.)

Army Form C. 2118

Place	Date	Hour	Summary of Events and Information	Remarks and references to Appendices
CORBIE	22.3.17	9.0.M	Cleaning arms, equipment and clothing. Horses in very muddy fields, but hope to find stables.	M
"	23.3.17		States found, continuance of cleaning	
"	24.3.17		Company training	
"	24.3.17		Company training. Lieut COMERY to Hospital, suspected measles	M
"	26.3.17		Lieut Bradbury rejoined	
"	27.3.17		Company training	
"	28.3.17		Company training	
"			Company training Dorfield Mulk no 1/1 DURHAM R.E.	M

vol 75

CONFIDENTIAL

WAR DIARY

OF

No 12 MACHINE GUN COMPANY

FROM 1st March 1917   To 31st March 1917

(VOLUMNE XV.) Lemman W for Captain
DE. No 12. M.G. COMPANY.

Army Form C. 2118

WAR DIARY
or
INTELLIGENCE SUMMARY
(Erase heading not required.)

Instructions regarding War Diaries and Intelligence Summaries are contained in F.S. Regs., Part II. and the Staff Manual respectively. Title Pages will be prepared in manuscript.

Place	Date	Hour	Summary of Events and Information	Remarks and references to Appendices
CORBIE	1/3/17	—	Company training carried out.	
"	2/3/17	—	Company training carried out.	
"	3/3/17	—	Company training carried out. Received Bde Operation Order for move on 4th inst.	
"	4/3/17	8·30 AM	Company marched out of CORBIE. Destination MONTONVILLERS, arrived MONTONVILLERS at 1·30 P.M.	
MONTONVILLERS	5/3/17	8·15 AM	Company marched out of MONTONVILLERS at 8·15 AM. Destination BEAUVAL arrived BEAUVAL at 2·0 P.M.	
BEAUVAL	6/3/17	9·0 AM	Company marched out of BEAUVAL at 9·0 A.M., Destination NOEUX. arrived NOEUX. at 2·40 P.M.	
NOEUX	7/3/17	10·0 AM	Company marched out of NOEUX at 10·0 AM. Destination BOUFFLERS. arrived BOUFFLERS. 1·10 P.M.	
BOUFFLERS	8/3/17	—	Company commenced cleaning arms, equipment etc. Continuation of cleaning &c.	
"	9/3/17	—	Continuation of cleaning commenced.	
"	10/3/17	—	Company training commenced. Band devices attached. 2 Lieut F. COMERY reports from Hospital	
"	11/3/17	—	Company training carried out.	
"	12/3/17	—	Company training carried out.	
"	13/3/17	—	Company training carried out.	
"	14/3/17	—	Company training carried out. Notification received of departure	

Captain BABER. J.B.

WAR DIARY
or
INTELLIGENCE SUMMARY
(Erase heading not required.)

Army Form C. 2118

Instructions regarding War Diaries and Intelligence Summaries are contained in F. S. Regs., Part II. and the Staff Manual respectively. Title Pages will be prepared in manuscript.

Place	Date	Hour	Summary of Events and Information	Remarks and references to Appendices
BOUFFLERS	14/3/17	9-0 AM	CAPT. J.B. BABER, left for GRANTHAM.	
"		2-0 P.M.	LIEUTS. T.R.T. LEASK, and J.H.C. DEVEY, reported from H.? Division School of Instruction. 2. O.R. Reinforcements.	
"	16/3/17	—	Company training carried out.	
"	17/3/17	—	Company training carried out.	
"	18/3/17	—	Company attend Church Services.	
"	19/3/17	—	Company training carried out. LIEUT. A. BLOOMFIELD joins company for duty as O.C. 1 O.R. reinforcements.	
"	20/3/17	8-0 AM	Company carry out training in conjunction with 2/Lester Regt.	
"	21/3/17	—	Company training during morning. 2/Lieut F. COMERY, and 1 O.R. proceed to MAGNICOURT as billeting party.	
"	"	2-00 PM	Limbers packed ready for move next day.	
"	22/3/17	8-0 AM	Transport move off. Destination ECOIVRES. Company march off at 10-20 A.M. to entraining point down of AUXI-LE-CHATEAU	
AUXI-LE-CHATEAU			arrive entraining point 12.30 P.M. Company entrained at 2-30 P.M. and moved off to MAGNICOURT. Company arrive CHELERS at 8-0 P.M. and	
CHELERS			march to MAGNICOURT arrive and settled in Billets by 10-0 P.M.	
MAGNICOURT.			heavy detailed for Stores not arrived at BOUFFLERS. Stores and 5. O.R. left Divroned.	
ECOIVRES			TRANSPORT. arrive ECOIVRES at 5-0 PM	
"	23/3/17		TRANSPORT depart ECOIVRES at 9-0AM Destination MAGNICOURT. arrive distination 11-0 A.M.	

Army Form C. 2118

WAR DIARY
or
INTELLIGENCE SUMMARY
(Erase heading not required.)

Instructions regarding War Diaries and Intelligence Summaries are contained in F. S. Regs., Part II. and the Staff Manual respectively. Title Pages will be prepared in manuscript.

Place	Date	Hour	Summary of Events and Information	Remarks and references to Appendices
BOUFFLERS	24/3/17	8 am	LORRY detailed to bring stores arrived. Stores loaded and LORRY proceed to MAGNICOURT arriving destination at 3·0 P.M.	
MAGNICOURT	25/3/17	—	Church services attended.	
— " —	26/3/17	—	Company training carried out	
— " —	27/3/17	—	Company training carried out.	
— " —	28/3/17	—	Company training as usual. C.O. (Captain Bloomfield) and 2 hunts 5 Company visit forward area, etc.	
— " —	29/3/17	—	Company training as usual.	
— " —	30/3/17	—	Company training as usual. Company view demonstration given by 1t T.M. Battery, trent heads and 2 OR visit forward area.	
— " —	31/3/17	—	Company training carried out.	

CONFIDENTIAL

WAR DIARY OF

No. 12 MACHINE GUN COMPANY.

FROM :- 1st April 1917   To 30th April, 1917.

(VOLUMNE. 14.)

Ern Semmer, Lt for Captain
OC No 12 Machine Gun Company

WAR DIARY

Army Form C. 2118

Place	Date	Hour	Summary of Events and Information	Remarks and references to Appendices
MAGNICOURT EN COMTE.	1/4/17	7-6 & 4-9 PM	Company training carried out. Brigade practice attack postponed until tomorrow.	RM
"	2/4/17	--	Company training carried out.	RM
"	3/4/17	--	Company route march postponed owing to heavy snowstorm. Box Respirator drill.	RM
"	"	2-9 PM	Conference at Brigade H.Q. for Section Officers with C.R.A.	RM
"	4/4/17	8-0 AM & 2-0 PM	Brigade training carried out. Instruction from Army Gymnastic School takes Officers and NCOs in Physical Training. Lieut Stage Dewey & 2nd AR proceed to forward area to reconnoitre Assembly Positions etc. Move on 6th inst postponed for 24 hours.	RM
"	5/4/17	--	Surplus blankets handed in. Move on 6th inst postponed for 24 hours.	RM
"	6/4/17	--	Operation Orders for move on 7th inst received from Brigade. Company Operation Orders for forthcoming Operations issued.	RM
"	7/4/17	--	Company marched out of MAGNICOURT EN COMTE at 9.30 AM Destination Y Camp. Arrived at 1-30 pm where GF MASON rejoined from M.G. School Camiers.	RM
Y Camp near ETRUN	8/4/17	--	Company organises ready for move to assembly area.	RM

WAR DIARY
or
INTELLIGENCE SUMMARY

Army Form C. 2118

Place	Date	Hour	Summary of Events and Information	Remarks and references to Appendices
Y. Camp	9/4/17	11-30 AM	Company (less transport and 25% reinforcements) marched off to assembly area under orders of Battalion Commander.	
G. 11.		2-0 PM	Captain A. BLOOMFIELD and HQ party proceed to forward Company HQ. Lieut-G.D.L. MONEY and 2 O.R. proceed to Company HQ. Lieut. J.H.T.C. DEVEY (OC 'C' section) slightly wounded. 1 O.R. wounded. Company HQ is established on BLUE LINE. 1 O.R. killed. 1 O.R. slightly wounded. Quiet night during which 'D' sections guns are established in houses at FAMPOUX, remainder in GREEN LINE, and 'A' section in dug-outs at HQ. Communication system with 1/Kings Own Royal Lancaster Regt.	
ATHIES	10/4/17	9-0 AM	Company HQ is moved from BLUE LINE to LA BAYETTE (qv). Situation quieter. Morning attack resumed in afternoon, but held up by rifle fire from hastily dug enemy trench. 'B' section give covering fire from left of Blue. 'B' and 'D' sections reach all enemy trenches with machine gun fire, owing to their being very shallow considerable damage was done. Enemy reported to be taking up position on Railway Embankment. Two Reserve guns under Lieut W.T.H. GRAINGER are established in a house about 100 yds in front of our line giving covering fire to VI Corps South of River SCARPE. Two enemy Machine Guns sniping detachments wiped out by reserve section guns. One of which was in a tree. Two men were seen to drop. One remains hanging. Line heavily bombarded during evening, quietening down at about 10-0 PM.	

WAR DIARY or INTELLIGENCE SUMMARY

Army Form C. 2118

Place	Date	Hour	Summary of Events and Information	Remarks and references to Appendices
line	10/4/17		Wounded 6 O.R.	PM
	11/4/17		Attack is continued with Cavalry ready to go through, but is again held up by Machine Gun fire. D. Section clear two trenches with enfilade fire apparently causing very heavy casualties. Heavy fighting around CHEMICAL WORKS. Hostile machine guns were refused to have been observed firing from house under cover of Red Cross flag. These Machine Guns were engaged by our own and Silenced. 1 O.R. killed 5 O.R. wounded	PM
	12/4/17		9th Division attack ROEUX - GAVRILLE Rd at 5.0 P.M. are reported to have gained objective but forced to retire owing to heavy casualties. 12th Brigade relieves during night. Section at Company HQ. (Reference 51/3 NW).	PM
	13/4/17		Sections proceed to G.11.	PM
	14/4/17	10-0 AM	Company HQ moves from Y bayete down to G.11. Line G.D. C. MONEY and 1 O.R. proceed to Y camp returning to G.11 at 8-0 P.M.	PM
G. 11.	15/4/17	10-0 AM	C.S. Mjr joins Coy HQ from Y Huts. Recd E.H. ROSE and 1 O.R. proceed to G.11	PM
	16/4/17	9-0 AM	Recd G.F MASON and 15 O.R's reinforcements join Company from Y Camp. Ammunition, Limbers, Rifles, Equipment etc thoroughly cleaned	PM

WAR DIARY
or
INTELLIGENCE SUMMARY

(Erase heading not required.)

Army Form C. 2118

Place	Date	Hour	Summary of Events and Information	Remarks and references to Appendices
G.H.Q.	17/4/17	—	Orders received for attachment of 2 sections to 102 Brigade for duties of Anti-aircraft work. Later order only 5 guns required.	
—	18/4/17	—	5 Guns under Lieut. J.R.T. LEASK and 2 Lieut W.J.H. GRAINGER moved to BROWN LINE to be attached to 102 Brigade.	
—	—	—	Company prepare to move up line.	
—	19/4/17	—	Brigade order cancelling all moves received	
—	20/4/17	9-0 AM	Orders for move next day to MONTENESCOURT. destination MONTENESCOURT. arrive there at 1-30 P.M.	
MONTENESCOURT	—	10-0 PM	Orders for move next day to MANIN. received	
—	21/4/17	9-15AM	Company leave MONTENESCOURT destination MANIN arrived there at 11-0 AM. Orders for move next day to BEAUFORT.	
MANIN	—	—	received from Brigade	
—	22/4/17	8-15	Company inspected by G.O.C. 18 Brigade prior to marching off to BEAUFORT. arrived BEAUFORT at 10-0 AM. Orders for move next day received	
BEAUFORT	23/4/17	—	Company left BEAUFORT at 10-0 AM. Destination LE CAUROY. arriving there at 12-0 noon	
LE CAUROY	24/4/17	—	Guns, Gun equipment, personnel equipment thoroughly cleaned. Company fired out	

WAR DIARY
or
INTELLIGENCE SUMMARY

Army Form C. 2118

(Erase heading not required.)

Place	Date	Hour	Summary of Events and Information	Remarks and references to Appendices
LE CAUROY	25/4/17	—	Company training carried out. Orders for move next day received	JM
—	26/4/17	—	Company left LE CAUROY at 9-15 A.M. destination SARS LE BOIS. Arrived Destination 11-0 A.M.	JM
SARS LE BOIS	27/4/17	—	Company move into billets east-end of village to make room for 1 Kings Own Regt. Orders to move next day received	JM
—	28/4/17	—	Company leave SARS LE BOIS at 9-40 A.M. destination TILLOY LES HERMAVILLE. arriving there at 1-30 P.M. Orders for move on 29th inst. received from Brigade	JM
TILLOY LES HERMAVILLE	—	—	13 O.R. Carriers join Company from HAN FOS	JM
—	29/4/17	—	Company leave TILLOY LES HERMAVILLE at 6-10 A.M. destination Shelter Camp H.13.b.4.7. arriving there at 11-30 A.M.	JM
G.11.	—	3.0 P.M.	Company erect Bivouacs and settle down for night.	JM
—	30/4/17	9-0 A.M.	Captain A. BLOOMFIELD and Lieut. E. ROGERS proceed to front line to reconnoitre positions etc	JM
—	—	7-0 P.M.	Conference at Brigade HQ for Commanding Officers	JM
—	—	9-15	Company moved to relieve 103. Machine Gun Company. Relief reported complete at 12-30 P.M.	JM

Vol 17.

CONFIDENTIAL

WAR DIARY

OF

No. 12 MACHINE GUN COMPANY

FROM 1st MAY 1917 To 31st MAY 1917

(VOLUMNE. XVII)

Guy D. Moray _____
O.C. No 12 Machine Gun Company

WAR DIARY
or
INTELLIGENCE SUMMARY

Army Form C. 2118.

Place	Date	Hour	Summary of Events and Information	Remarks and references to Appendices
H24 b.	1/5/17	—	Situation in line fairly quiet. Several bursts of shell fire.	Pm
	2/5/17	—	Situation still quiet. Preparations for attack made. ZERO hour is at 4.0 am on 3rd inst. Company HQ moves to Quarry at Lyons H18.c.2. at 9.30 pm.	Pm
			Notification received of award of "Military Medal" to Sgt Corless, and "Bar to Military Medal" to Sgt Ashurst.	
FAMPOUX	3/5/17		Attack commenced. Heavy casualties. 14 OR killed, hints E.Rogers, G.T. Mason and T.E. Andrews, and 23 OR wounded. 5 OR missing, 2 guns damaged, and 2 guns lost. During the attack 8 Lewis guns turnage on CEMETERY at I 19.d.	Pm
	4/5/17		Company HQ at Quarry. Heavily shelled. Several casualties. Coy HQ moved from Quarry. 15 German +B system have reach J.R.T. & 2.5 OR's reinforcements from SAVY proved to Company HQ.	Pm
	5/5/17		Coy Sgt Mgr Mercedo 15 O in Company HQ. Damages lump and down to transport. One gun on ack aircraft work in u.S. German system. Positions dug on 4th system for defence.	Pm
	6/5/17		Company reorganised into 12 teams, 2 hrd hunter 'King' One Lyt Guns Company for Lanspart duties, lost Company Kinfeld 16 [town] Company 3rd Q	Pm

WAR DIARY or INTELLIGENCE SUMMARY

Army Form C. 2118.

Place	Date	Hour	Summary of Events and Information	Remarks and references to Appendices
	7/5/17		4 Guns in front line relieved by 51st Bn Company. These 4 guns after relief proceed to Quarry and relieve 4 guns of ROTA & 4 Guns which return to Bn HQ.	PM
	8/5/17		Positions in Sunken Road reconnoitred by Captain G.D.C. MOTLEY. Proceeds to transport lines. Casualties for 12 guns to barrage on ROEUX cemetery. Railway Embankment and Sunken Rd.	PM
	9/5/17	4 PM	4 Guns to Quarry. Orders to breakdown 16 breakdowns, carrying party sent from Company HQ. Breakdowns completed without a hitch. Section reorganised.	PM
	10/5/17	9 PM N. M 3.0 AM	Sections move to positions in Sunken Rd & in road N. of 3 giving and commence improving positions. Battery of French etc. C.O. visits by G.O.C. Brigade not to move bay H.Q. whereconnected in N of Syllion	PM
	11/5/17	10 to 4.30	Company HQ are ordered to move to Old BLUE line railway embankment. 4 forward machine gun officers. Officers of Divisional HQ moves to transport lines.	PM
		2.0 AM	Company HQ moves to transport lines.	PM
		7.30 AM	ZERO hour. Barrage successful. 4 guns target Blue nd: 1 OR Killed, 9 OR wounded. Attack successful. Objectives gained.	PM

Army Form C. 2118.

WAR DIARY
or
INTELLIGENCE SUMMARY.
(Erase heading not required.)

Place	Date	Hour	Summary of Events and Information	Remarks and references to Appendices
	12/5/17	6:30 AM	Attack resumed. Huns again put down barrage on positions of importance. Attack successful all objectives gained.	7 m
G.17.		10 pm	Company relieved and proceed to Lyons G.17. Orders for move on 13/5/1917 issued.	P.m
	13/5/17	11:30	Company arrive Line Hot meal provided for them on arrival. Shell in trench.	P.m
		5:0 AM	Reveille. Transport moves off at 5:45 AM. Rest Company 7 & 2 OR billeting party moves at 6:0 AM	P.m
		9:0 AM	Company moves off to advancing point at G.21.B.6.8. and proceed to PENIN. Transport arrive PENIN	P.m
PENIN.	14/5/17	11:30 PM	Company arrive 2:30 PM.	
			Kit and Gun equipment Inspection. Lieuts MUTCH. F.P, METCALF. R BURBOROUGH. R.W. & BROADHEAD. L.R + 35 OR reinforcements join Company. 4 OR from SAVY rejoin.	P.m
	15/5/17	—	Company training. Carried out. 30 OR reinforcements arrive.	P.m
	16/5/17	—	Men who took part in recent attack inspected by 3rd Army Commander.	P.m
		2:30 PM	Company Baths at Tingues. Notification received of Capt BLOOMFIELD D.S.O. having been awarded a Military Cross. E. H. ROSE	P.m

Army Form C. 2118.

WAR DIARY
or
INTELLIGENCE SUMMARY

(Erase heading not required.)

Place	Date	Hour	Summary of Events and Information	Remarks and references to Appendices
PENIN.	17/5/17	—	Company training carried out.	PM
—	18/5/17	—	Company training as usual.	PM
—	19/5/17	—	Company training as usual. 2 O.R. to U.K on leave.	PM
—	20/5/17	—	Company attend Divine services. Company kits inspected by G.O.C. Division. 2 Lieut MUTCH. A.W. + 13 OR to SAV9 on anti-aircraft duties	PM
—	21/5/17	—	Company route march. 10 O.R. to U.K. on leave. Lieut COMERY F. to Abbeville attend Course of Transport duties	PM
—	22/5/17	—	Company training carried out. Captain BLOOMFIELD A. to U.K on leave. Lieut G.D.C. MONEY assumes command of Company.	PM
—	23/5/17	—	Company training carried out. 1 O.R. to U.K. on leave. Inter-section relief. 2 Lieut METCALF. R. + 13 OR returns anti-aircraft section at SAV9. Company training as usual.	PM
—	24/5/17	—		PM
—	25/5/17	—	Corps Commander presents medal ribbons to Officers N.C.Os. and men of Brigade who have been awarded same. C.S.M WARD. S. + Sgt ALDHURST G. receives Bar to "Military Medal". Lieut E. H. ROSE to U.K on leave.	PM
—	26/5/17	—	Company training carried out	PM

Army Form C. 2118.

WAR DIARY
or
INTELLIGENCE SUMMARY.
(Erase heading not required.)

Instructions regarding War Diaries and Intelligence Summaries are contained in F. S. Regs., Part II. and the Staff Manual respectively. Title pages will be prepared in manuscript.

Place	Date	Hour	Summary of Events and Information	Remarks and references to Appendices
PENIN	27/5/17	—	Divine Service attended. 1 O.R. proceeds to U.K. on leave.	
—	28/5/17	—	Heut W/H Grainger proceeds to U.K. on leave. 2/Lt Bunborough and + 13 O.Rs proceed to SAVY to relieve 2/Lt R. Metcalf + 13 O.Rs doing anti-aircraft duties. Relief completed by 6-0 P.M.	P.m P.m
—	29/5/17	—	Company training carried out. Officers attend lecture on new method of Bayonet fighting + Physical Training	P.m P.m
—	30/5/17	—	Brigade sports takes place. 2 O.Rs to U.K. on leave	
—	31/5/17	—	Company training carried out.	

Vol 18.

CONFIDENTIAL

WAR DIARY
OF
No 12 MACHINE GUN COMPANY

FROM 1st June 1917 To 30th June 1917

(VOLUME 18)

Shearer Lieut. for Captain
Commanding No 12 Machine Gun Company

30/6/1917

Army Form C. 2118.

WAR DIARY
or
INTELLIGENCE SUMMARY.
(Erase heading not required.)

Instructions regarding War Diaries and Intelligence Summaries are contained in F.S. Regs., Part II. and the Staff Manual respectively. Title pages will be prepared in manuscript.

Place	Date	Hour	Summary of Events and Information	Remarks and references to Appendices
PENIN.	1/6/1917	9-0 AM	Divisional Horse Show takes place. Company transport enter 2 events. 25 O.R.s of company are taken by lorries to show ground.	
		11-0 AM	Transport win 2nd Prize in event No 2. 10R proceeds on leave to U.K. 2Lt BROADHEAD + 13 OR D section where 1 Lt. BURBOROUGH + 13 OR	
		2-0 PM.	'C' section on Anti aircraft duties at SAVY.	
	2/6/1917	9-0 AM	Company training carried out.	
		2-0 PM	Recreational training.	
	3/6/1917	10-0 AM	Divine services attended	
	4/6/19	9-0 AM	Company training as usual. Captain A. BLOOMFIELD, M.C. rejoins from leave to U.K. Corps Machine Gun Officer visits company. 1 OR proceeds to U.K. on leave.	
	5/6/1917	9-0 AM	Company training carried out. G.O.C. 4th Division visits company. Team for Brigade Rifle meeting selected.	
	6/6/1917	9-0 AM	Company training as usual. Practice rifle shooting etc. on range preparatory for Brigade tournament. 10R to U.K. on leave	
	7/6/1917	9-0 AM	Bayonet fighting teams, shooting teams exercised under Lieut. SAYERS.	

Army Form C. 2118.

WAR DIARY
~~INTELLIGENCE SUMMARY~~
(Erase heading not required.)

Place	Date	Hour	Summary of Events and Information	Remarks and references to Appendices
PENIN	8/10/17	9.0 AM	Teams for Shooting, Bayonet & Bullet Competition practice on Range	
DOFFINE FARM		11-0 AM	Company attend presentation of Medal Ribbons by Divisional Commander to Captain BLOOMFIELD "Military Cross", Lieut E.H. ROSE "Military Cross", 10748 R/C ASHWORTH. J. "Military Medal", 10792 P/C THOMPSON. F. "Military Medal".	
PENIN	9/10/17	6.30 AM	Filling Bulls & taking limbers ready for move in the evening.	
		10-0 AM	Brigade Rifle Meeting Commences. Company wins 1st and 2nd Prizes in Machine Gun Competition	
		11-0 AM	Lieut. G. D. C. MONEY. M.C. proceeds to M.G. School, Camiers.	
		6-0 PM	Transport moves off to Forward Area. Anti-Aircraft Section at SAVY relieved by Yorkshire Hussars.	
		7-0 PM	Buses arrive to convey Company to Forward Area.	
		10-0 PM	Company arrive ARRAS and are settled in Billets	
		12 MN	Transport arrives ARRAS.	
ARRAS	10/10/17	9-0 AM	Captain BLOOMFIELD. M.C., and C.S.M. proceed to 27th Coy HQ at FAMPOUX to arrange relief.	

WAR DIARY
INTELLIGENCE SUMMARY

(Erase heading not required.)

Army Form C. 2118.

Place	Date	Hour	Summary of Events and Information	Remarks and references to Appendices
ARRAS	10/5/17	11-30 P.M.	Company move off by sections at 5 minute intervals to relieve 2½ of M.G. Coy in the line. Company H.Q. is established in cellars in FAMPOUX by 7-0 P.M. Relief report complete at 10-40 P.M. Situation fairly quiet.	J.H.
"	11/5/17		Situation normal. Intermittent shelling on both sides. Enemy aircraft very active, burn fire 2,000 rds at three from CRETE TRENCH. 2 Lieut W.J.H. GRAINGER wounded.	J.H.
"	12/5/17		2 Lt R. METCALF and 1 OR wounded. Captain BLOOMFIELD M.C. visits line positions. Our artillery systematically shell enemy front system & shell holes from 12 noon till 12-15 P.M. 2 Lieut W.J.H. GRAINGER joins Coy H.Q. M.O. visits Brigade to discuss situation with G.O.C. Brigade. 2 teams of A section and 2 teams of B section are withdrawn from front line, and are established in gun pits West of Fampoux. These guns do anti-aircraft work.	J.H.
		9-0 P.M.		

Army Form C. 2118.

WAR DIARY

~~INTELLIGENCE SUMMARY~~

(Erase heading not required.)

Instructions regarding War Diaries and Intelligence Summaries are contained in F.S. Regs., Part II. and the Staff Manual respectively. Title pages will be prepared in manuscript.

Place	Date	Hour	Summary of Events and Information	Remarks and references to Appendices
Front line	13/6/17	—	Situation normal. Major LOW M.C., D.M.G.O. visits Coy H.Q. C.O., along with D.M.G.O. visits positions in line. From 2.30 p.m till 10-0 p.m enemy occasionally shelled the CHEMICAL WORKS, CHATEAU, and RAILWAY	SR
"	14/6/17	—	Company H.Q shelled. 1 Gun knocked out by a direct hit, and 1 O.R wounded. From 9-0 A.M. enemy shelled Cross Roads W. end of FAMPOUX intermittently. 1 O.R. killed	SR
"	15/6/17	—	Enemy Artillery shelled positions intermittently. 2nd in Command visits Gun positions in line. 2 Guns in support open fire on enemy Aircraft driving them back to their own lines. Lieut F. COMERY rejoins from Transport Course ABBEVILLE. 1 O.R proceeds to 27th M.G. Company. 1 O.R rejoins from leave. 1 O.R wounded. Situation fairly quiet.	SR
"	16/6/17	—	Situation normal. Officers of relieving Company reconnoitre Gun positions. Company H.Q Heavily shelled.	SR
		10pm	Coy H.Q moves from FAMPOUX to Dug-outs at H.17.C.2.6.	

WAR DIARY
or
INTELLIGENCE SUMMARY.
(Erase heading not required.)

Army Form C. 2118.

Place	Date	Hour	Summary of Events and Information	Remarks and references to Appendices
In the Line	10/9/17	—	I.O.R. returned from leave. Situation fairly quiet.	[sig]
—	11/9/17	—	Situation normal. L.O. visits gun positions in line. FAMPOUX shelled intermittently during day.	[sig]
—	12/9/17	—	Preparations for relief made. Situation normal in line.	
		6.0 PM	Relieving company arrive. Relief carried out smoothly. Coy H.Q. & Brigade H.Q. heavily shelled.	
		8.0 PM	Our Artillery shell enemy front line and system of shell holes	
		9.0 PM	Coy Transport arrives to convey guns etc to FIFE CAMP. Sections move off in small parties.	
		9.30 PM	Relief reported complete.	
		10.30 PM	Company arrive out and are settled in tents at FIFE CAMP. Notification received that 1 hour have to take up positions in Intermediate line.	
FIFE CAMP		9.0 AM	Captain BLOOMFIELD M.C. and C.S.M. proceed to reconnoitre positions in "Intermediate line"; teams proceeding to positions in line are provided with a test and dress change.	[sig]

Army Form C. 2118.

WAR DIARY
or
~~INTELLIGENCE SUMMARY~~
(Erase heading not required.)

Instructions regarding War Diaries and Intelligence Summaries are contained in F. S. Regs., Part II. and the Staff Manual respectively. Title pages will be prepared in manuscript.

Place	Date	Hour	Summary of Events and Information	Remarks and references to Appendices
FIFE CAMP	10/10/17	14.45	2Lieut. BROADHEAD, L.R in charge of detachment of 7 guns proceed to line, Arrive and are settled in positions at LANCER LANE, and GAVRIELLE SWITCH. Night passes off quietly	✓
—	21/6/17		Lieut. H. BRADBURY rejoins from leave to U.K. Company training carried out. Overhauling, cleaning of guns and gun equipment.	✓
—	21/6/17		Company drill as usual. 1 O.R. to U.K. on leave.	✓
—	22/6/17		Company training carried out. Lieut W.J.H. GRAINGER rejoins from Corps Depot SAVY. Later Section relief takes place 2Lt A.W. BURBOROUGH, in charge of 2 teams of A, 2 teams 'B' and 3 teams 'C' section relieve 2Lt BROADHEAD L.R. + detachment in LANCER LANE, and GAVRIELLE SWITCH. Relief completed by 10-0 P.M.	✓
—	23/6/17		Lieut N. MACVIE joins Company from M.G Base depot otherwise uneventful.	✓
—	24/6/17		Divine service attended. Captain BLOOMFIELD. M.C, Lieuts H BRADBURY, GRAINGER. W.J.H, and 2Lt BROADHEAD. L.R	✓

Army Form C. 2118.

WAR DIARY
or
INTELLIGENCE SUMMARY.
(Erase heading not required.)

Place	Date	Hour	Summary of Events and Information	Remarks and references to Appendices
FIFE CAMP	24/10/17	10·0 AM	FIFE proceed to hire to reconnoitre positions prior to taking over from 118 M.G. Company. 1 O.R. proceeds to UK on leave.	H
	25/10/17	9·0 AM	Company training as usual. 2 Teams of A Section and 2 Teams of 'B' Section are withdrawn from "Intermediate hire". Arrive at Company HQ FIFE CAMP at 10-30 PM.	H
		9·0 PM	Cleaning of Guns and Gun equipment.	
	26/10/17	9·0 AM	Lieuts W.H. GRAINGER and N. MACVIE with No 13, 15, and 16 teams proceed to hire to relieve Guns of 118 M.G. Company. 2nd Lieut F.P. MUTCH proceeds to relieve 2/Lt R.W. BURBROUGH in the "Intermediate hire"	H
		5·0 PM	Captain A. BLOOMFIELD M.C. and 2/Lt L.R. BROADHEAD proceed to 352 M.G. Company HQ to reconnoitre positions and make friends arrangements re relief.	H
	27/10/17		Preparations for move into hire made	

WAR DIARY
or
INTELLIGENCE SUMMARY

Army Form C. 2118.

Place	Date	Hour	Summary of Events and Information	Remarks and references to Appendices
FIFE CAMP H35 d.5.9.	27/6/17	7.45PM	Company moves off. Halt for ¼ of an hour at RITZ Dump where a guide is met to take Company to 35th Company HQ.	ff
"		9.45PM	Arrive at Coy HQ and pick up guides to convey teams to positions in the line. Situation normal.	ff
"	28/6/17	1.0AM	Relief Completed.	
"		4.0AM	Enemy Aeroplane brought down by one of our Triplanes, crashes into its own lines. Situation normal. Work carried out:- Improvement of trenches, gun emplacements etc.	
"		10.3PM	Captain BLOOMFIELD. M.C. visits all positions in line. Weather very wet. 1 OR wounded (accidentally) 1 OR leave to U.K.	ff
"	29/6/17	4.0AM	D.O. arrives back to Coy HQ from visiting positions in line. Situation normal	
"		2.0PM	C.O. visits LOC 12th Brigade.	
"	30/6/17	4.0PM	Situation normal, weather dull showery.	
"		9.0PM	C.O. along with GOC Brigade, and Divisional commander visits gun positions in line. Orders for inter-relation relief to take place on issued. Situation normal	ff

WAR DIARY
or
INTELLIGENCE SUMMARY

Army Form C. 2118.

Place	Date	Hour	Summary of Events and Information	Remarks and references to Appendices
	30/4/17	—	Lieut G. D. C. MONEY. M.C. rejoins from M.G. school Cruises. Lieut F. COMERY rejoins from leave to UK.	

Vol 19.

CONFIDENTIAL

WAR DIARY

OF

No 12 MACHINE GUN COMPANY

FROM 1st July 1917.   To 31st July 1917

(VOLUMNE XIX.)

Guy Demoray M Roy
Captain
Commanding No 12 Machine Gun Company

28/1917

Place	Date	Hour	Summary of Events and Information	Remarks and references to Appendices
H.35.d.5.9.	1/7/1917	—	Situation normal. Relief carried out in the following order:- No 15 Team to Coy H.Q. No 13 +16 Teams to LANCER LANE. Lieut GRANGER W.J.H. to Coy H.Q. No 9 Team and Lt F.P. MUTCH to Coy H.Q. 14 Teams under Lieut M. MACVIE relieve Lieut H. BRADBURY and 4 Teams. after relief Lieut H. BRADBURY and his four Teams take over positions in Relief reported complete at 3-30 A.M. Company H.Q. shelled intermittently between midnight and 3-0 A.M. Situation Quiet. Enemy put a few high Aerial torpedos and rifle grenades about FINGER Trench and RIFLE trench between 1-0 and 2-0 A.M. K and L posts shelled at irregular intervals. Intermittent shelling round Company H.Q. 1 direct hit in Gun pit. R.E.'s working on M.G. dug-out in FINGER TRENCH report that they can hear enemy working near by.	JM
—	2/7/17	—	Situation normal. 5 ORs reinforcements join Company.	JM

Army Form C. 2118.

WAR DIARY
~~INTELLIGENCE SUMMARY~~

(Erase heading not required.)

Instructions regarding War Diaries and Intelligence Summaries are contained in F. S. Regs., Part II. and the Staff Manual respectively. Title pages will be prepared in manuscript.

Place	Date	Hour	Summary of Events and Information	Remarks and references to Appendices
H35.d.9.5	2/1/17	8.0 AM	Enemy put a few shells into MONCHY. Heavy artillery barrage on ROEUX and CHEMICAL WORKS lasting about 20 minutes. E.A. engaged by Machine Gun fire. An enemy Machine Gun traversed LANCER LANE, causing working party to take cover. Two enemy signalling lamps observed in use at about PARK WORK and REGENT WORK.	(M)
		6.0 PM	Two aeroplanes observed shewing no wing markings but both having black tails. I.O.R slightly bombarded. Company H.Q heavily shelled. B.O visits at duty. Company at Rougeur H.Q. G.O.C. 12th Bde at Rougeur H.Q. Situation very quiet. Boisdeville artillery activity on right of our area. H36.a and H35.b shelled with 5.9.	(O)
	3/1/17	2.15 PM	LONE LANE and LANCER LANE shelled heavily. During the attack on our right, the enemy lights were observed as follows:- RED - single bursting into three. Orange - single. Green single. B.O visits line area selects gun positions	(O)

Army Form C. 2118.

WAR DIARY
or
~~INTELLIGENCE SUMMARY~~

(Erase heading not required.)

Place	Date	Hour	Summary of Events and Information	Remarks and references to Appendices
H.35 & 9.5	4/7/1917		Lieut G.D.C. MONEY M.C. proceeded to U.K on leave.	
"	5/7/1917		Situation normal. Slight artillery activity on our right. One of our triplanes flew very low over the enemy lines. Intermittent shelling by enemy.	
"	6/7/1917	6-AM	Our artillery very active during night. Enemy trench mortars very active on our front line. Several enemy aircraft flew over our lines. 1 O.R. killed, 1 O.R. wounded by trench mortar. A small red balloon was sent over from	
		3-15.AM	the enemy lines, apparently with a message. It fell about I.31.a. central. LANCER LANE shelled.	
"	7/7/1917		Situation normal. Our artillery again very active during the night. 3 Enemy aircraft flew over our lines at	
		7-30 AM	but were driven back by anti-aircraft fire. ORANGE trench flown in by trench mortars close beside our gun position. Strait was made for enemy	

Army Form C. 2118.

WAR DIARY
or
INTELLIGENCE SUMMARY.
(Erase heading not required.)

Instructions regarding War Diaries and Intelligence Summaries are contained in F.S. Regs., Part II. and the Staff Manual respectively. Title pages will be prepared in manuscript.

Place	Date	Hour	Summary of Events and Information	Remarks and references to Appendices
H35 d9.5	7/7/1917		red balloon which dropped on 6th inst, but was unable to find it. An E.A. flew over our lines and dropped a white light, when in reply the enemy artillery on our right opened fire.	
		9.30 AM	Situation normal. B.O. visits line positions in line at 9-30 P.M. and returns at 2-0 A.M. Artillery very quiet. Enemy Trench Mortar very active about 9-0 A.M. Enemy aircraft again very active. 3 OR reinforcements join Company	
	7/7/17 8/7/17			
	9/7/17		Situation normal. Enemy shelled area round Company HQ intermittently. B.O. visits gun positions of 12th Division fifteen to an Operation leaving Coy HQ at 9-0 PM and returning at 1-0 A.M. Our artillery fairly active. Enemy Dump exploded by our guns during the night. Enemy sniped again. Seen about 11-45° P.M. at Corner of PELVES LANE. B.O. visits the HQ of 35th M.G. Company.	
	14/7/17		Situation very quiet. Inter section relief carried out and completed at 2-0 AM	

Army Form C. 2118.

WAR DIARY
or
INTELLIGENCE SUMMARY
(Erase heading not required.)

Instructions regarding War Diaries and Intelligence
Summaries are contained in F.S. Regs., Part II.
and the Staff Manual respectively. Title pages
will be prepared in manuscript.

Place	Date	Hour	Summary of Events and Information	Remarks and references to Appendices
H35 d 5	10/4/17		During the night the enemy put a large number of shells Gas, in Valley EAST of LANCER LANE	M
"	11/4/17		LONE LANE shelled intermittently. Enemy active during the night with rifle grenades. 2 E.A. flying over our lines are engaged by our M.G's. Enemy Machine Guns and Trench Mortars fairly active.	M
"	12/4/17		Situation normal, artillery activity during afternoon. Our artillery shell enemy support and reserve line, Box Barrage from 10-50 P.M. to 11-0 P.M. One of our aeroplanes was forced down by E.A. about 5-50 P.M. Plane landed S.W. of MONCHY. Between 6 + 8 P.M. both E.A. and Our Aircraft flew low over front lines. E.A. were driven off by our M.G. fire.	M
	2-30pm		Junction of Rifle and Chain trench bombarded with Trench Mortar shells.	
"	13/4/17		Situation fairly quiet E.A. very active 3 E.A. flew low over our front lines about 7-30 A.M.	M

WAR DIARY

(Erase heading not required.)

Army Form C. 2118.

Place	Date	Hour	Summary of Events and Information	Remarks and references to Appendices
H35 d.9.5	12/7/17		Situation normal. Our Artillery very active during afternoon. Orders re relief of Company by 112th M.G. Coy received. Relieving Company arrive at 11.0 PM.	
	13/7/17		Relief complete at 3.0 AM. Company move in small numbers to FIFE CAMP. Company being in Divisional reserve. Company rest during day.	
FIFE CAMP			Overhauling and cleaning of Guns	
	14/7/17	3.0 PM	Company in training. Continuation of cleaning guns and equipment	
		2.0 PM	Bathing Parade.	
	15/7/17		Divine Services attended. Lieut. Q.D.C. MONEY, M.C. rejoins from leave.	
	16/7/17	8.0 AM	Company proceed with a hot bath and clean change of underclothing	
		10 AM	Company less transport leave FIFE CAMP and move to G.24 c.9.1 where tents are erected and improvements on Camp carried out.	
G.24 c.9.1				

Army Form C. 2118.

WAR DIARY

Instructions regarding War Diaries and Intelligence Summaries are contained in F. S. Regs., Part II. and the Staff Manual respectively. Title pages will be prepared in manuscript.

(Erase heading not required.)

Place	Date	Hour	Summary of Events and Information	Remarks and references to Appendices
Gu.Cq.	17/7/17	—	Continuation of improvements to Camp, Shell hole filled in, bath house erected, anti gas appliances inspected. GOC 12th Brigade visits Camp.	M
—	18/7/17	12 noon	Company training carried out. Lieut A.W BURBOROUGH and Lieut J.R.T LEASK admitted to Hospital sick. Lieut proceeds to U.K. on leave.	M
—	19/7/17	—	Company training as usual, otherwise uneventful.	M
—	25/7/17	—	'B' Section attacked 15 ? train End for training in tactical exercise. Remainder of Company training as usual.	M
—	21/7/17	9am	Company tactical exercise carried out.	
—		2-0PM	Recreational training	M
—	22/7/17	8-30AM	Camp heavily shelled, Company take cover in cellars of ruined Château. Divine services cancelled. Company paid out at 2-0pm.	M

WAR DIARY

Army Form C. 2118.

Place	Date	Hour	Summary of Events and Information	Remarks and references to Appendices
G 24 C.9.	22/1/17	—	Orders received from Brigade of 6 Guns to proceed on 24th inst. to relieve 6 Guns of 9th Division doing Anti-aircraft duty on Ammunition Dumps & Railway Station at SAVY, and ROELLE COURT. Orders for move of Camp received.	
"	23/1/17	5.0AM	Camp struck and conveyed by transport to new area MIDDLESEX CAMP.	
		6.30AM	Commenced to pitch Camp.	
			Orders came to personnel proceeding to relieve Anti-aircraft guns of 9th Division.	
		1.0PM	Orders re Sub-Section proceeding to SAVY on Anti-aircraft duty cancelled.	
	24/1/17	8.0AM	Lieut W.J.H. GRAINGER and C section proceed to ROND POINT ARRAS where they entrain and are conveyed to ROELLE COURT, and LIGNY-ST-FLOTCHEL. Relief of 4 Guns of 9th Division completed at 1.0PM.	

Army Form C. 2118.

WAR DIARY
or
INTELLIGENCE SUMMARY.
(Erase heading not required.)

Instructions regarding War Diaries and Intelligence Summaries are contained in F.S. Regs., Part II. and the Staff Manual respectively. Title pages will be prepared in manuscript.

Place	Date	Hour	Summary of Events and Information	Remarks and references to Appendices
Gr.eq.	24/1/17	9.0 AM	Remainder of Company proceed on route march. Improvements on camp carried out.	fm
"	25/1/17	-	Company training carried out, Pickets after still. Lieut S.C. SIM and 2/Lieut A.C. WARD join Company. D.M.G.O. visits Company.	fm
"	26/1/17	-	Company training as usual. Lieut G.D.C. MONEY M.C. gives a lecture on Barrage fire.	fm
"	27/1/17	-	Company training under Lieut STORER.	fm
		2.0 PM	Swimming Parade.	
		7.0 PM	Captain A. BLOOMFIELD M.C. receives notification of relief to take place on 28th inst.	
"	28/1/17	9.0 AM	C.O. & C.S.M.s visits relief. The 112th Machine Gun Company H.Q. to arrange relief. Guns cleaned and limbers packed ready for move into line.	fm
			No. 1 Section under Lieut W.J.H. GRAINGER leaving	

WAR DIARY
or
INTELLIGENCE SUMMARY.
(Erase heading not required.)

Army Form C. 2118.

Place	Date	Hour	Summary of Events and Information	Remarks and references to Appendices
G.H.Q.1	2/7/17	1.0 PM	Anti-Aircraft duty at ROELLECOURT are relieved by a Section of 234 M.G. Company after relief C Section is brought to Company in Motor Lorries.	Pm
		7.45 pm	Company less D Section proceed by Motor Company H.Q is established at 10 P.M. Heavy artillery fire from 10.45 P.M. to 11-30 P.M. when guns quieten down	Pm
	24/7/17	1.0 AM	Relief reported Complete Captain Bloomfield assumes command of guns in 111th Brigade Sector. Situation normal. Heavy thunderstorm at 10-30 AM lasts about half an hour. Artillery Enemy intense activity in the vicinity of LONE TRENCH. MONCHY shelled at intervals during the night. Enemy M. guns traversed along CHAIN and RIFLE trenches at intervals. At 5.45 AM 6 Enemy Aeroplanes appeared over our lines, these were dispersed by A.A. Guns and eventually driven off by our planes	Pm
		2.0 PM	L.O. along with I.O. in Command visits Gun positions in the Line	

Army Form C. 2118.

WAR DIARY
or
INTELLIGENCE SUMMARY.
(Erase heading not required.)

Instructions regarding War Diaries and Intelligence
Summaries are contained in F. S. Regs., Part II.
and the Staff Manual respectively. Title pages
will be prepared in manuscript.

Place	Date	Hour	Summary of Events and Information	Remarks and references to Appendices
	30/7/17		At 2-30 AM until 4-30 AM FINGER Trench was subjected to heavy fire. M. Gun position was slightly damaged. During the night our Machine Guns fire on PELVE'S LANE and DEVIL'S Trench about I.32.a.10.15. 3000 Rds were fired.	An
		2-0 PM	N.O.4 Second-in-Command visits positions in the line.	
		4-0 PM	A heavy T.M. Dump exploded about I.31.6.15.85. Three men R.G.A were killed	
	31/7/17		Enemy Artillery fired bursts every 15 minutes between 12 MN and 3-30 AM. MONCHY & vicinity shelled intermittently during the evening. Machine Guns (our) carried out indirect fire on enemy lines and tracks. Trench Mortars (enemy) active on our front line. Emplacement constructed at Bdy HQ for indirect fire. Lieut A.C. WARD admitted to hospital. Signaling was again observed in the direction of PLOUVAIN	An

Vol 20

CONFIDENTIAL

WAR DIARY

OF

No 12 MACHINE GUN COMPANY

FROM 1st August 1917   To 31st August 1917

(VOLUMNE XVIII)

Guy Somers, Captain
Commanding No 12 Machine Gun Company

Army Form C. 2118.

WAR DIARY
or
INTELLIGENCE SUMMARY

(Erase heading not required.)

Place	Date	Hour	Summary of Events and Information	Remarks and references to Appendices
Trenches MONCHY SECTOR	1/8/17	12 M^N 3-30 PM	Enemy Artillery fired bursts about every 15 minutes. Occasional shells were put into MONCHY. Trench Mortars were active on front line during the early hours of the morning. Our Machine Guns carried out indirect fire on roads and tracks used by the enemy. Number of Rounds fired 6,000 Rds. 2 Lieut A.C. WARD. admitted 16 Hospital sick.	P.m
		9-30 PM	Signalling was again observed in direction of PLOUVAIN. Our artillery fairly quiet during day, but commenced firing bursts at 9-30 p.m. Enemy shells CHAIN TRENCH and damaged No 4 M.G. position. Captain BLOOMFIELD. M.C. visits all guns positions in line.	
	2/8/17		An Artillery quiet until about 6-0 P.M. when they turned on enemy trenches opposite the castle on our right. Enemy Artillery very active during the whole day. About 9-0 P.M several green lights were sent up by the enemy, on which the Artillery fire commenced. RIFLE and CHAIN TRENCH received	P.m

Army Form C. 2118.

WAR DIARY
INTELLIGENCE SUMMARY

(Erase heading not required.)

Place	Date	Hour	Summary of Events and Information	Remarks and references to Appendices
MONCHY AREA	Sunday 2/9/17		Our Machine Guns carried out Harassing fire throughout the night on enemy tracks and road. Number of rounds fired :- 2,300. I.O. visits all positions in the line. Hostile machine guns were active during the night especially from direction of JIG-SAW WOOD.	P.M
	3/9/17		Enemy continued our usual fire heavily during the early hours of morning. Our Machine Guns in CHAIN and RIFLE Trench open out in response to S.O.S. signal going up from destn on our right. Dropping barrage was again observed in direction of DELBAR WOOD at 6-40 P.M. and 11-45 P.M. At 11-45 P.M. enemy sent up an Amber light which burst into about 150. Nothing special followed.	P.M
		8.0 PM	I.O. along with Lt. BROADHEAD visit gun positions. Our Machine Guns Carried Out Harassing fire on enemy tracks & roads etc. Number of rounds fired 2,300.	

WARY DIARY
INTELLIGENCE SUMMARY

Army Form. C. 2118.

Place	Date	Hour	Summary of Events and Information	Remarks and references to Appendices
Trenches Monchy Aux	18/1/17	—	In the early morning an enemy working party was seen between PELVES and JIG-SAW WOOD, it was dispersed by our Machine Gun fire.	
		9.30 AM	G.O. visits Brigade H.Q.	
		2.0 PM	Lieut. G.D.C. MONEY. M.G. visits gun position in the line. Hostile Artillery very quiet during day; a few 5.9's fell on LANCER LANE and S of C. Post. Our Machine Gun in RIFLE trench cooperates with T.M.B. in firing on suspected O.P. on M.G. in ANGEL trench I 25. d.7.3. apparently with good effect. A number of 5.9's dropped in the vicinity of Bay H.Q. Enemy trenches opposite our sector were shelled intermittently by our Artillery with 6" Hows: during the day. From 10.0 P.M. to 10.15 P.M. they bombarded the enemy trenches and approaches with guns of all calibres.	

Army Form C. 2118.

WAR DIARY
or
INTELLIGENCE SUMMARY.
(Erase heading not required.)

Instructions regarding War Diaries and Intelligence
Summaries are contained in F. S. Regs., Part II.
and the Staff Manual respectively. Title pages
will be prepared in manuscript.

Place	Date	Hour	Summary of Events and Information	Remarks and references to Appendices
MONCHY AREA	4/9/17		During the night our Machine Guns fired the usual harassing fire on Enemy Tracks & roads. Number of rounds fired 2,560.	
	5/9/17		At about 1.0 AM — 1.30 AM Our Artillery appeared to be using gas or smoke shells, as a haze which was visible was left over the enemy's lines from 2.15 PM 2.30 PM enemy shell Bay HQ with 4.1's and 5.9's.	
		8.0 PM	Later Divison relief takes place D Section B Section who when relieved proceed to Crowfoot Caves.	
		10.20 PM	Enemy shell MONCHY with 5.9's and the ground in the vicinity of No 4 Gun was subjected to heavy shelling. Enemy Machine Guns traversed RIFLE trench and about Q and H Posts during the night. Harrassing fire again Carried out by our Machine Guns on Enemy tracks & roads. Number of rounds fired 2,600.	

Army Form C. 2118.

WAR DIARY
or
INTELLIGENCE SUMMARY
(Erase heading not required.)

Place	Date	Hour	Summary of Events and Information	Remarks and references to Appendices
Trenches	6/8/17	3-0 PM	Enemy T.Mortars very active about FINGER Trench and CHAIN Trench. Enemy Artillery quiet during the day. MONCHY was shelled during the morning. From 3-0 PM to 6-0 PM ORCHARD was shelled with 5.9" shells and shrapnel. 70o and trench in Ervillers Trench shelled with 4.2"	pm
MONCHY AREA		11.30 PM	BAYONET Trench shelled with 4.2" Our Machine Guns carried out harassing fire on Enemy tanks tracks. Number of rounds fired 2,970. Enemy Machine Guns were fairly active during the night. RIFLE and SCABBARD Trench were swept at intervals. Trench Mortars (Stokes) were active in front of FINGER and CHAIN Trenches	
"	7/8/17	10 AM	Our Machine Guns in FINGER TRENCH fired on men observed an enemy working party who were in front of their trench. Machine Guns (ours) gave the usual harassing fire. Number of rounds fired 31,925.	pm

Army Form C. 2118.

WAR DIARY
or
INTELLIGENCE SUMMARY
(Erase heading not required.)

Instructions regarding War Diaries and Intelligence Summaries are contained in F. S. Regs., Part II. and the Staff Manual respectively. Title pages will be prepared in manuscript.

Place	Date	Hour	Summary of Events and Information	Remarks and references to Appendices
Trenches MONCHY AREA.	7/9/17	1-0 PM	Our Artillery shelled the enemy front and support trenches. Our Artillery replied to the S.O.S. signals going up north of the river. Artillery (enemy) fairly quiet. E. Machine Guns active RIFLE and SCABBARD trenches during the night. Our A.P.A. drove off 3 E.A. flying over our lines. D.M.G.O. 12th Division visits Bay'n H.Q. 2.O. & 2nd-in-Command visit all gun positions. Final arrangements re Staffa 8th inst. issued. Staffa taking place 8 inst postponed 24 hours. Orders re this - decision reby issued.	pm
—	8/9/17		Our Artillery shelled DEVILS trench, but ceased about 11-0 PM. H.Q. Artillery more active following places being shelled :- MONCHY, LONE LANE, ORCHARD trench. HALBERD trench was badly damaged in parts, and entrances to dug-outs in CURB LANE were blown in	pm

WAR DIARY
or
INTELLIGENCE SUMMARY

(Erase heading not required.)

Army Form C. 2118.

Place	Date	Hour	Summary of Events and Information	Remarks and references to Appendices
Trenches HONGH AREA	3/8/17		Machine Guns (enemy) fire harassing fire throughout the night. Number of rounds fired 2,150. Enemy M.Gs fire bursts during night. Enemy Trench Mortar was observed to be firing from DEVIL'S WOOD. Fire was brought to bear on it same it did not fire again. Signalling was observed in the direction of DELBAR WOOD.	
	4/8/17		Our Artillery heavily bombarded the enemy front line trench DEVILS WOOD during the whole day. Hostile artillery did not retaliate very heavily. Enemy however until ZERO hour, when a heavy barrage 8.15pm was put down on front and support trenches. ELBOW, FINGER and SCABBARD trenches were badly damaged in several places. ORCHARD trench was heavily shelled between 7.45 P.M. and 8.45 P.M.	

Army Form C. 2118.

WAR DIARY
or
INTELLIGENCE SUMMARY.

(Erase heading not required.)

Place	Date	Hour	Summary of Events and Information	Remarks and references to Appendices
Sereeke – MONCHY AREA.	9/8/17		Machine Guns Ours fired bursts from ZERO – 11½ hrs to ZERO – 67 minutes, when firing increased in intensity and remained intense until ZERO + 1 hour when it eased off. Machine Guns fired 591,000 Rds during the course of Operations. One of the guns in HALBERD stand engaged two enemy machine guns, ultimately leaving the effect of their fire. Another gun in same stand with the LING succeeded in hitting many of the enemy on the left of the tanks "eola", particularly in left flank where the enemy appeared to rush when our bombardment lifted. This two gun fired 30,000 to harassing fire was carried out during the night. 2,1050 being fired. Enemy Machine Guns were very active during the whole night. Artillery on both sides were fairly quiet. Our Artillery shelled DEVILS trench for a few minutes during the afternoon.	M
	10/8/17			M

Army Form. C. 2118.

WAR DIARY
or
~~INTELLIGENCE SUMMARY~~

(Erase heading not required.)

Instructions regarding War Diaries and Intelligence Summaries are contained in F.S. Regs., Part II. and the Staff Manual respectively. Title pages will be prepared in manuscript.

Place	Date	Hour	Summary of Events and Information	Remarks and references to Appendices
Lendre MONCHY AREA	14/8/17		Enemy shelled BIT LANE, and junction of CURB and RIFLE trench. Our machine guns gave the usual harassing fire during the night. 3500 rds being fired. One of our Observation Balloons broke loose during the evening and drifted over the enemy lines, where it was brought down by two E.A. 6 Hostile Balloons went up. Two of these were shelled by our long range guns, and very puffed down. Our Artillery was fairly active during the day. Enemy fired several bursts of 10 cm shells on LONE LANE, RIFLE SUPPORT, and SCABBARD trench.	M
	14/8/17		C.O. and Second in-Command visit Gun positions in the line. Our Machine Guns gave harassing fire throughout the night, firing 4,000 Rds. Enemy M.G's were less active than usual. Enemy shelled CHAIN, FINGER, and ELBOW trenches with trench mortars	M

WAR DIARY
or
INTELLIGENCE SUMMARY

(Erase heading not required.)

Army Form C. 2118.

Place	Date	Hour	Summary of Events and Information	Remarks and references to Appendices
Trenches	11/8/17	—	A signalling lamp was Observed in DELBAR WOOD and VICTORIA Copse, the signals were a white light followed by what appeared to be the Morse Code.	(M)
MONCHY AREA	14/8/17	—	Artillery of both sides were fairly quiet during the whole day. About 7-8 PM a fire was caused to the east of DELBAR WOOD. Harassing fire again carried out by our Machine guns. Numbers of rounds fired 3,300. Enemy M.G's fairly quiet. Hostile aircraft were more active than usual during the day.	(M)
	15/8/17	—	Orders for relief issued. Situation normal.	(M)
		12 N	Our Machine Guns carry out harassing fire firing 2,850 Rds	
		3-30 PM		
		9-30 PM	Relieving Company arrive & are met by guides at Dump. Relief carried out and Completed by 11-30 P.M. After relief Company proceed to DINGWALL CAMP	

Army Form C. 2118.

WAR DIARY
or
INTELLIGENCE SUMMARY.
(Erase heading not required.)

Place	Date	Hour	Summary of Events and Information	Remarks and references to Appendices
DINGWALL CAMP	14/8/17	2-30 AM	Company arrive in Camp, Hot meal is provided for them on arrival.	pm
"	15/8/17	10-A.M.	Cleaning of guns and equipment. Inspection of Gun equipment etc, in the afternoon.	pm
"	16/8/17	—	Company Cleaning of Guns, Fitting steel helmets. Inspection of Auto Gun Appliances. Steel Helmet drill. Recreational Training	pm
"	17/8/17	2.PM	Company drill, training carried out. Binders worked.	pm
"	18/8/17	2PM	Swimming parade. Company training as usual, otherwise uneventful	pm
"	19/8/17	—	Company attend Divine Service. Instruction received by Capt Schonfeld M.C. being appointed Instructor at the Lewis Gun School. Lieut Q.	pm

Army Form C. 2118.

WAR DIARY

(Erase heading not required.)

Place	Date	Hour	Summary of Events and Information	Remarks and references to Appendices
DINGWALL CAMP.	20/8/17	—	Company training carried out. Camp and field still been.	—
	21/8/17	—	Fatigue party of 60 men found to unload coal at ARRAS station. Remainder of Coy carry out training.	—
		10.0 PM	Capt. A. BLOMFIELD M.C. heut. G.H.Q. School. Capt. G.D.C. MONEY. M.C. assumed command of company. and heut. H. BRADBURY takes over the duties of second in command.	—
	22/8/17	—	Company training carried out as usual.	—
	23/8/17	—	Company training. Anti-gas appliances inspected by O.C. Gas N.C.O. Lieut. S.G. SIM admitted to hospital.	—
	24/8/17	—	Officers witness tactical scheme by the King's Own R.L. Regt. Company on fatigue building new stone standings on new transport lines.	—

Army Form C. 2118.

WAR DIARY
or
INTELLIGENCE SUMMARY.

(Erase heading not required.)

Place	Date	Hour	Summary of Events and Information	Remarks and references to Appendices
DINGWALL CAMP	25/8/17	—	Company again on Fatigue building new Horse Standings at Brigade Transport Lines. Otherwise uneventful.	PM
— " —	26/8/17	—	Company attend Divine Service. Notification received Attachment of Lieut G.D.O. MONEY. M.C. 16 Tournament The Company.	PM
— " —	27/8/17	—	Company Bathing Parade in the morning. Fatigue Party to Strong found to work on Brigade Transport Lines. Captain G.D.O. MONEY. M.C. attends Gas course in the morning. "C" section carry out training under Section Officer.	PM
— " —	28/8/17	—	Company training under Lieut. STORER. O.O. again visits Gas Course. Lt. S. CLARKE gives Demonstration with YUKON PACK. Company turn out in the evening	PM

Army Form C. 2118.

WAR DIARY
or
INTELLIGENCE SUMMARY
(Erase heading not required.)

Place	Date	Hour	Summary of Events and Information	Remarks and references to Appendices
DINGWALL CAMP	29/8/17		Company carry out cleaning of guns and looking Lewkers ready for move into line for relief.	
		9:0 AM	Capt. MONEY M.G. visits 11th M.G. Coy HQ to arrange details for relief.	
		7.15 P.M.	Company march off for Trescho. Company HQ arrive at 9-30 P.M. Relief reported complete by 11-50 P.M. Situation normal.	
Trescho MONCY AREA	30/8/17		Artillery fairly quiet during the day. BOIS DUSART was shelled in the morning and DELBAR WOOD during the evening. Enemy shelled MONCHY and ORCHARD RESERVE at intervals. Our Machine Guns fire harassing fire during the night. Number of Rds fired: 3500 Enemy Machine Guns fairly quiet. One appeared to be firing from the direction of BOIS DES AUBERINES to Orvais Gun positions in the line.	

Army Form C. 2118.

WAR DIARY
or
INTELLIGENCE SUMMARY.
(Erase heading not required.)

Instructions regarding War Diaries and Intelligence Summaries are contained in F. S. Regs., Part II. and the Staff Manual respectively. Title pages will be prepared in manuscript.

Place	Date	Hour	Summary of Events and Information	Remarks and references to Appendices
Jerusalem MONCHY AREA	31/8/17		Our artillery fired occasional bursts throughout the day at 7.0 PM a few shells were dropped near the N edge of J.6. SAP WOOD. Enemy artillery showed increased activity during the day. Our Machine Guns carried out harassing fire on enemy tracks, roads etc during the night.	PM
		9.0 PM	Number of Rounds fired "2,400" on hostile gun positions	PM

CONFIDENTIAL   M.21.

WAR DIARY

OF

No. 12 MACHINE GUN COMPANY

FROM 1st September 1917   To 30th September 1917

(VOLUMNE XXI)

Rm Summers   Captain
Commanding No 12 Machine Gun Company

1/10/917

Army Form C. 2118.

WAR DIARY
or
INTELLIGENCE SUMMARY
(Erase heading not required.)

Instructions regarding War Diaries and Intelligence Summaries are contained in F. S. Regs., Part II. and the Staff Manual respectively. Title Pages will be prepared in manuscript.

Place	Date	Hour	Summary of Events and Information	Remarks and references to Appendices
Trenches MONCHY AREA	1/9/1917	—	Situation normal. Our Machine Guns fired harassing fire throughout the night. Number of rounds fired 2,600. Hostile Machine Guns were less active than usual, a few bursts were directed on LANCER and LEMON AVENUE	#B
		5·0 PM	A small party of the enemy was seen to leave the left edge of JIG SAW WOOD.	#B
			C.O. visits all Gun positions	
—	2·9·17	—	Situation fairly quiet. Our artillery fairly active during the morning	#B
		12 noon.	Enemy shell front and support lines. Our Machine Guns give usual harassing fire on enemy lines of approach etc; firing from 9·30 P.M. to 3·30 A.M. Number of rounds fired 2,400.	#B
			Hostile Machine guns were fairly active. C. and H. posts were harassed several times throughout the night.	#B
		8·0 PM	C.O. visits gun positions in the line.	#B
			Interdiction relief takes place. A Section relieves B Section.	

WAR DIARY
or
INTELLIGENCE SUMMARY

Army Form C. 2118.

Place	Date	Hour	Summary of Events and Information	Remarks and references to Appendices
Trenches MONCHY AREA	3/9/17	—	Situation normal. Our Machine Guns fired in co-operation with the artillery and also harassing fire on enemy tracks etc. 7 Targets were engaged and 4,900 rounds were fired. Hostile M.G's were less active than usual. A Machine Gun traversed RIFLE TRENCH several times during the night. Signalling was observed on the left of JIG SAW WOOD situated in the line fairly quiet. An enemy shell LEMON Avenue & MUSKET TRENCH with H.2.s	
	4/9/17	—	Our Machine were again very active, firing in cooperation with Artillery. 6 targets were engaged, and 5,700 Rds were fired. Lieut H BRADBURY attends F.G.C.M. convener for the trial of Sergt WRIGHT. S.O. visits gun positions in the line.	
	5/9/17	—	Situation in the line normal. Our machine guns were again very active during the night, firing 6,200 rds. Artillery of both sides fairly quiet. S.O. visits Lewis gun positions in the line. S.O. of the 43rd M.G Coy	

Army Form C. 2118.

WAR DIARY
or
INTELLIGENCE SUMMARY
(Erase heading not required.)

Instructions regarding War Diaries and Intelligence Summaries are contained in F.S. Regs., Part II. and the Staff Manual respectively. Title Pages will be prepared in manuscript.

Place	Date	Hour	Summary of Events and Information	Remarks and references to Appendices
Tenders MONCHY AREA	5/9/17	2-5PM	Batt Coy HQ to arrange detail for relief taking place on night 7th and 8th inst. Situation in the line remains quiet.	#62
	6/9/17	—	Our Machine Guns fire harassing fire throughout the night on enemy tracks and roads. Number of Rds fired 5,700. Hostile Machine Guns were fairly quiet. Occasional bursts being fired on support trenches. Company orders to relief taking place next day came to hand. 6.0 units positions in the line. Lieut H. BRADBURY proceed to transport lines to prepare for relief. Guns of relieving company are brought up and staked at Coy HQ. 1 man per team accompanying the gun equipment. Situation normal.	#63
	7/9/17	—	Our Machine Guns again give harassing fire on enemy lines of approach, firing 5,300 Rds. One man per team of the relieving company is	#64

2449 Wt. W14957/M90 750,000 1/16 J.B.C. & A. Forms/C.2118/12.

Army Form C. 2118.

WAR DIARY
or
INTELLIGENCE SUMMARY

(Erase heading not required.)

Instructions regarding War Diaries and Intelligence Summaries are contained in F. S. Regs., Part II and the Staff Manual respectively. Title Pages will be prepared in manuscript.

Place	Date	Hour	Summary of Events and Information	Remarks and references to Appendices
Trenches MONCHY AREA	7/9/17	—	attached to the gun teams on the line, for purpose of handing over.	H.Q
		4-0PM	O.O. visits gun positions in the line. Our guides meet relieving Company at FAMPOUX LOCK, and guide them to Coy H.Q. where they pick up guns equipment & proceed to line to relieve 12th Machine Gun teams. Relief complete at 8-0 P.M. Gun limbers arrive at Dump at 8-30 PM and convey guns etc. to Transport Lines. Company proceeds to LEVI BARRACKS where they are billeted for the night. Hot meal provided on arrival. Orders for move early next morning issued. Reveille 3-30AM. Limbers packed and Company ready to move off by M. Ward route 15 new Area by 7-0 AM.	
ARRAS	8/9/17	5-0AM		H.Q
BLAIREVILLE CAMP No 2		9-60	Company arrive new Camp. Bathing for Company provided at BLAIREVILLE. 2Lt C.H. ASPHAR and 3 O.Rs joined Company from Base	
	9/9/17	—	Company attend Divine Services. Conference at Brigade H.Q for O.Os	H.Q

Army Form C. 2118.

WAR DIARY
or
INTELLIGENCE SUMMARY.
(Erase heading not required.)

Instructions regarding War Diaries and Intelligence Summaries are contained in F.S. Regs., Part II. and the Staff Manual respectively. Title pages will be prepared in manuscript.

Place	Date	Hour	Summary of Events and Information	Remarks and references to Appendices
BLAIRVILLE CAMP.No.2	10/9/17	—	Company training commences including Immediate action & Bolt filling whilst wearing gas masks. Route march (Rapid marching) and Barrage fire drill	X3
—	11/9/17	—	Company training same lines as for 10th inst.	X3
—	12/9/17	—	Company training continued. Afternoon Quarter-artillery drill. Company Football team play 1/King's Own Regt. Won 3 goals to 2.	X3
—	13/9/17	—	Usual Company training carried out. Company Football team play 21st West Yorks in 1st Round Brigade Championship. Lose 6 goals to nil. C.O. reconnoitres field firing range prior to Tactical scheme which takes place on 14th inst. Company Operation Orders for Tactical scheme issued. 10 Officers conversant.	X3
—	14/9/17	3.0 PM	Company taking at BLAIREVILLE	X3
—	—	—	Company training again carried out. (Brigade warning Order Received)	
—	15/9/17	2.0 PM	Tactical scheme for Offrans length.	
—	—	—	Company Football team play 23rd Manchester Result Draw. Divisions observed	X3

Army Form C. 2118.

WAR DIARY
or
INTELLIGENCE SUMMARY
(Erase heading not required.)

Instructions regarding War Diaries and Intelligence Summaries are contained in F. S. Regs., Part II. and the Staff Manual respectively. Title pages will be prepared in manuscript.

Place	Date	Hour	Summary of Events and Information	Remarks and references to Appendices
BAIRSWILLE CAMP No 2	16/9/17	-	'A' Company attend Divine Services	
	10/9/17	10 AM	'A' Company football team play 234 M.G. Coy. Result:- Draw	
	17/9/17	-	Company training carried out. Orders for move received	
	18/9/17	-	Carry out cleaning of guns, and packing limbers preparatory to move next day. 1 O.R. reinforcement joins Company. Lieut. S.G. SIM and 1 OR proceed to new area as advance billeting party. Company orders for move next day issued. Reveille at 5-0 A.M. Fatigues cleaning Camp and carrying stores.	
	19/9/17	6.0 AM	Transport move off separately to railhead. Company horse and mule off to railhead at BEAUMETZ-RIVIERE. Horses and vehicles entrained by 9-30 A.M. Troops entrained by 9-55 A.M. without mishap. Train moves off at 10-0 A.M.	

Army Form C. 2118.

WAR DIARY
or
INTELLIGENCE SUMMARY
(Erase heading not required.)

Instructions regarding War Diaries and Intelligence Summaries are contained in F. S. Regs., Part II. and the Staff Manual respectively. Title pages will be prepared in manuscript.

Place	Date	Hour	Summary of Events and Information	Remarks and references to Appendices
PESEL HOEK	10/9/17	7.20	Arrive Re-training station PESEL HOEK at 7.20 P.M. Company and Transport detrained. Lieut S.E SIM meets Company to guide them to billetting area. Transport moves off under Bergn. arrangements. Company arrive and are billetted in tents at SASKATOON CAMP.	
SASKATOON CAMP	11/9/17	2-0AM	Transport arrive	
		9-0 AM	Improvements in Camp and Transport lines carried out. Y.O.C 12th Inf Brigade visits Camp.	
—	2/9/17	—	Company training carried out during the morning. 2 Guns mounted on Anti-Aircraft duty in the afternoon. Improvements in Camp & Lines carried out.	
—	23/9/17	—	Company training again carried out.	
		5-0PM	Conference for all Commanding Officers at Bde Head[quarters] etc	

Army Form C. 2118.

WAR DIARY
or
INTELLIGENCE SUMMARY.
(Erase heading not required.)

Place	Date	Hour	Summary of Events and Information	Remarks and references to Appendices
SASKATOON CAMP	23/9/17	—	Company attend Divine Services	
	24/9/17	—	Orders received for party to proceed to the line to reconnoitre positions	
		9 am	Company training during the morning. Divisional Commander Inspects units of 12th Bde on their respective Parade grounds	
		4.30 PM	C.O., Lieut E.H ROSE M.C. Lieut S.G. SIM proceed to forward area by buses to reconnoitre positions	
	25/9/17	—	Company route out. Company training as usual.	
		2 PM	Baths attended 15 Company.	
		2.30 PM	C.O. and Lieuts ROSE and SIM arrive back from forward area.	
	26/9/17	—	Company training. Overhauling of guns and gun equipment. Lieut H BRADBURY proceeds to forward area to make arrangements for relief	

Army Form C. 2118.

WAR DIARY
or
INTELLIGENCE SUMMARY.
(Erase heading not required.)

Place	Date	Hour	Summary of Events and Information	Remarks and references to Appendices
SASKATOON CAMP	24/9/17	2.0 PM	C.O. attends a conference at Brigade H.Q. Brigade Operation Order Received. Lieut. BRADBURY returns from the line. Company Operation Order for move next day issued.	A/3
	24/9/17		Company parade 9.50 AM and move off to entraining point INTERNATIONAL CORNER, entraining complete by 11.45 A.M.	A/3
		12 noon	Transport move off separately to new Transport lines under orders of Transport Officer. Company arrive at ELVERDINGHE, where they detrain and march to WOOLF CAMP. Tea provided for men before moving off to the line. 25% Company under Lieut. E.H. ROSE, M.C. proceed direct to DRAGON CAMP. "A" Section (Reserve Section) proceed to Transport lines	
WOOLF CAMP		5.45	"B", "C", "D" sections H.Q. move off to positions in the front	

Place	Date	Hour	Summary of Events and Information	Remarks and references to Appendices
Trenches	28/9/17	6-0 PM	Guides are met at BARDS CAUSEWAY to guide sections to Company HQ. Guns, Rations, Water etc conveyed from there round to Boy HQ on trolleys. Arrive Coy HQ at 9 p.m. Guides are met here to take reliefs to positions in the line. B section remains in support at Company HQ. Relief reported completed by 11-30 p.m. Situation fairly normal. Continuous artillery activity on both sides. Enemy Machine guns very quiet. Heavy shelling round WHITE HOUSE.	X
—	29/9/17	6-0 AM	LIEUT H. BRADBURY arrives at Coy HQ to take command. Captain G.D.C. MONEY proceeds to Transport lines sick. Artillery again very active. 1 O.R. slightly wounded.	X
—	30/9/17	12 MN	Intn section relief takes place. B section relieves C section. D section relieves A section relieves D section, proceeding to Transport lines	X

Army Form C. 2118.

WAR DIARY
or
INTELLIGENCE SUMMARY.
(Erase heading not required.)

Place	Date	Hour	Summary of Events and Information	Remarks and references to Appendices
Trenches LANGEMARCK AREA	20/11/17		Desultory shelling by enemy artillery during morning, increasing in activity towards noon. Machine Guns fairly quiet.	

CONFIDENTIAL

WAR DIARY

OF

No 12 MACHINE GUN COMPANY

FROM 1st OCTOBER 1917   To 31st OCTOBER 1917

(VOLUME XXII)

JnoStewart Lieut
Commanding No 12 Machine Gun Company

WAR DIARY
or
INTELLIGENCE SUMMARY.
(Erase heading not required.)

Army Form C. 2118.

Instructions regarding War Diaries and Intelligence Summaries are contained in F. S. Regs., Part II. and the Staff Manual respectively. Title pages will be prepared in manuscript.

Place	Date	Hour	Summary of Events and Information	Remarks and references to Appendices
Trenches	1/8/17	—	Artillery Activity on Front Line. Brigade Operation Orders for relief next day received. Situation normal.	
—	2/10/17	—	Officers of Relieving Company visit positions to take over. Company Orders for relief issued. Company H.Q. very heavily shelled. "C" Section H.Q. partly blown in at 5.30 p.m. Repaired to SOLFERINO CAMP. "A" & "B" sections relieved by 1 section each of 10th and 11th M.G. Companies. Relief reported complete by 11.30 p.m. Sections after relief proceed to SOLFERINO Camp. 2 teams of "A" lost the way.	
SOLFERINO CAMP	3/10/17	—	Cleaning of guns & gun equipment carried out. 2 teams of "A" rejoin after being lost all night. Cleaning & improving Camp during the afternoon.	
—	4/10/17	—	Captain A.D.C. MONEY rejoins from hospital. Lieut J.R.T. Keark rejoins from M.G. School. G. + Q. C.O. attends a conference at Coulogne H.Q.	

Army Form C. 2118.

WAR DIARY or INTELLIGENCE SUMMARY

(Erase heading not required.)

Place	Date	Hour	Summary of Events and Information	Remarks and references to Appendices
SOLFERINO CAMP	14/9/17	—	Orders received from Brigade for 1 Section & relieve 1 section 11th M.G. Company & 3 guns in support. Lieut S.G. SIM proceed to line to reconnoitre position.	XO
— " —	15/9/17	—	Physical training carried out in the morning. 8 ORs per Section gun Battery for the following Operations. A Section under 2nd Lt. F.D. MUTCH & 3 guns under Lieut H. MACVIE proceed to the line to relieve guns of the 11th M.G. Company. These sections were their guns & relieved W.J H. GRAINGER & despatched to find them. Relief complete at 11-30 p.m. 1 OR wd & 1 OR missing. Lieut S.G. SIM proceed to C. Camp to join the details.	XO
— " —	16/9/17	—	Sections are allotted to Battalions as follows A Section to 1/Kings Own C Section 2/Essex B " " 1/Rifle Brigade D " " 2/West Riding	XO

A5834. Wt. W4973/M687 750,000 8/16 D.D. & L. Ltd. Forms/C.2118/13.

WAR DIARY
or
INTELLIGENCE SUMMARY.
(Erase heading not required.)

Army Form C. 2118.

Place	Date	Hour	Summary of Events and Information	Remarks and references to Appendices
SOLFERINO CAMP	4/10/17	—	Company Operation Orders for attack issued. Captain MONEY proceeds to line to arrange details of Relief. Lieut. J.R.T. LEASK accidentally sprains his ankle & is admitted to hospital. 2nd Lt. C.H. ASPHAR takes Command of B Section vice Lieut LEASK. A hot meal is sent to the sections already in the line. Sections proceed to the line under Battalion orders. Remainder of Company move from SOLFERINO Camp to the transport lines. Relief reported complete by 11.0 P.M.	
LINE	5/10/17		Captain MONEY proceeds to line Company H.Q. is established at DOUBLE COTS. Situation normal	

WAR DIARY
or
~~INTELLIGENCE SUMMARY.~~

(Erase heading not required.)

Army Form C. 2118.

Place	Date	Hour	Summary of Events and Information	Remarks and references to Appendices
LINE	9/10/17	—	Attack commenced at 5-20 P.M. Lieut W.J.H. GRRINGER and Lieut C.H ASPHAR wounded 2 ORs killed 14 ORs wounded 1 OR missing	HD
"	10/10/17	—	Consolidation of position gained. 1 gun blown up 1 damaged & 1 lost. Artillery very active	HD
"	11/10/17	—	Lieut COMERY proceeds to the line, and takes Command of the 2 guns attached to the 2nd West Ridings at present in Reserve at JOLLIE FARM. These guns move into position at 5-0 PM	HD
"	12/10/17	—	Captain MONEY returns to Transport Lines Dick Captain CORBALLIS O.C. 11th M.G. Company takes Command of guns in the line. Orders for relief next day received. Attack again takes place	HD
"	13/10/17	—	Preparations for relief made. 2 Teams of C & D Sections arrive at LEIPZIG Coup. No accommodation is available so they are billeted at transports lines	HD

WAR DIARY
or
INTELLIGENCE SUMMARY

Place	Date	Hour	Summary of Events and Information	Remarks and references to Appendices
	13/10/17	—	Hot meal provided for them on arrival. Remainder of Company under Lieuts MACVIE and COMERY arrive from line at 8-0 a.m.	
	14/10/17	—	Transport moves off to new area at POINT CAMP Company parade at 9-30 a.m. Moved to entraining point at ELVERDINGHE entraining at 11-30 a.m. and detrain at PROVEN and march to POINT CAMP Company is billeted in Barns. Muster parade held at 3-0 p.m.	
POINT CAMP	15/10/17		Company further cleaning guns & gym equipment, washing bunkers etc. 5 ORs reinforcements join Company. 25 ORs reinforcements under Lieut E.H. ROSE. join Company. Lieut F.P. MUTCH proceeds to U.K. on leave. Orders for next day received	
"	16/10/17		Company parade 9-45 a.m to be informed off to	

WAR DIARY or INTELLIGENCE SUMMARY

Army Form C. 2118.

Place	Date	Hour	Summary of Events and Information	Remarks and references to Appendices
ST-JAN-TER-BIEZEN	16/10/17		Arrive at ROAD CAMP at 1-15 P.M. Company billets in Marquis. Lieut. G.M. BENNETT joins Company to Command. Lieut. J.R.T. LEASK rejoins from Hospital. 10 ORs reinforcements join Company.	XB
-"-	17/10/17		Company parades. C.O's inspection. Cleaning & overhauling of Gun Equipment. 2 Lieut. J.L. ROGERS joins Company. Orders for move next day received.	XB
-"-	18/10/17		Company Operation Orders for move 18th inst issued. C.O's inspection. Surplus Stores taken to entraining station. Cleaning camp prior to evacuation carried out. Transport moves off at 2-0 p.m. Company moves off 4-30 p.m. Entrain at HOUT POTRE railhead at 7-0 P.M.	XB

Army Form C. 2118.

WAR DIARY
or
INTELLIGENCE SUMMARY.
(Erase heading not required.)

Place	Date	Hour	Summary of Events and Information	Remarks and references to Appendices
	18/10/17		Train moves off at 7-32 PM	A9
AUBIGNY	19/10/17	7-30 AM	Arrive & detrain at AUBIGNY at 7-30 AM. Lorry convoys surplus stores to MOYELETTE. Company arrive 8-30 AM. Billets cleaned. Company training carried out. Inspection of kit & gun equipment.	A9
MOYELETTE	20/10/17		Company attend Divine Service	A9
"	21/10/17		Company training carried out	A9
"	22/10/17		Numbers washed & taken. Administrative instructions for move on 2nd met received.	A9
	23/10/17		Company training in billets owing to bad weather. 2 M2s proceed to new area to take over billets	A9
"	24/10/17		Company orders for move next day issued. Limber packed stores & blankets stacked ready. Move off at 12 noon	A9

WAR DIARY
or
INTELLIGENCE SUMMARY

Army Form C. 2118.

(Erase heading not required.)

Place	Date	Hour	Summary of Events and Information	Remarks and references to Appendices
OUELETTE	24/10/17		Lieut S.G. SIM & 10 OR proceed on bicycle in advance party	
			Company made move off at 2.20 P.M	
			Arrive ARRAS & installed in billets at 6.30 P.M	X9
			Company HQ is at 34 Rue Frederic Debergo	
			Transport lines and Men billets at RONVILLE	
ARRAS	25/10/17		Company inspected by OC.	
			Practice on Range from 9.30 AM to 1-0 P.M	X9
		2.0 PM	Cleaning guns filling belts.	
			OC's Conference at Brigade HQ.	
	26/10/17		Company training carried out.	X9
			Lieut E.H ROSE proceeds to U.K. on leave	
	27/10/17		Company training as usual	X9
			Fatigue Party of 110 ORs found for work on Rue	
			Liverpool Line	
			2Lt J.L Rogers & 1 gun team proceed to HORSE SHOE	X9
			DUMP for Anti-Aircraft duties	

Army Form C. 2118.

WAR DIARY
or
INTELLIGENCE SUMMARY
(Erase heading not required.)

Place	Date	Hour	Summary of Events and Information	Remarks and references to Appendices
ARRAS	1/10/17	—	Company attend Divine Service. Otherwise uneventful	XI 9
"	2/10/17	—	Company training as usual. 2 Lt F.P. HUTCH rejoins from leave.	XII 9
"	3/10/17	—	Company training parade at SCHRAMM Barracks afterwards continuation of Company training	XIII 9
"	3/10/17	—	Training carried out as usual.	XIV 9

WA 23

CONFIDENTIAL

WAR DIARY

OF

No 12 Machine Gun Company

From 1st November 1917 To 30th November 1917

(Volumne XXIII)

AmSmith
Captain
Commanding No 12 Machine Gun Company

WAR DIARY or INTELLIGENCE SUMMARY

Army Form C. 2118.

Place	Date	Hour	Summary of Events and Information	Remarks and references to Appendices
ARRAS	1/4/1917		Company Training carried out. 2 Lieut. J.R. STANWAY joins Company. Continuation of Company Training.	BHR
"	2/4/17		Afternoon. The Gun & team on Anti-aircraft duty at Horse Shoe Dump fired by the L.F's.	BHR
"	3/4/17		R.C's attend Divine service at Catholic Club. 10.0 proceeds to 11th M Gun Coy H.Q at BROWN LINE to arrange details for relief. Returns at 3.0 p.m. Lieuts SIM & MACVIE attached 163rd R.F.A. for 3 days instruction in co-operation between artillery machine gun fire.	BHR
"	4/4/17		Company attend Divine service in Billets. C.O. attends conference at Bde. H.Q. Lieut. LEASK & 2 Lt. BROADHEAD proceed to the line to reconnoitre position.	BHR
"	5/4/17		Company training carried out. Company Question Returns to M.G. Base. Surplus to establishment. 2 Lt J.R. STANWAY proceeds	BHR

Army Form C. 2118.

WAR DIARY
INTELLIGENCE SUMMARY
(Erase heading not required.)

Place	Date	Hour	Summary of Events and Information	Remarks and references to Appendices
ARRAS	6/11/17	—	Continuation of Company receiving final orders for move next day base. Limbers packed ready to proceed to line.	DWR
—	7/11/17	—	Limbers proceed to line at intervals of 20 minutes. Limbers are unloaded at H.Q. where guides are met to take Guns to positions. A Guns in front system, 4 guns of B section in support at Bay H.Q. 3 Guns of C section remain at ARRAS under Lieut. SIM & Lieut. J.L ROGERS. Relief completed by 6.0 P.M. Situation in the line normal.	DWR
LINE N + b.20.d3	9/11/17		C.O. visits all gun positions. Situation normal. Lieut ROSE. M.C. returns from leave & proceeds to join Division on right. Carry out a raid & our guns cooperate in Barrage fire. Machine guns give overhead fire on enemy tracks. No of Rounds fired 91,000 Rds.	DWR

WAR DIARY
or
INTELLIGENCE SUMMARY

Army Form C. 2118.

(Erase heading not required.)

Place	Date	Hour	Summary of Events and Information	Remarks and references to Appendices
LINE M4 & 9048	9/11/17		CO along with D.M.G.O. visits all positions in the line. Situation fairly quiet.	OR
— " —	10/11/17		Hostile T.M. fire on CANNISTER & HILL support. Our Machine guns very active during the night, firing 10,100 R.ds on enemy lines.	OR
— " —	11/11/17		Situation normal. Enemy Machine Guns more active. CO visits gun positions. Machine Guns fire 11,500 R.ds on enemy positions.	
— " —	12/11/17		Situation fairly quiet. CO. & D.M.G.O proceed to line, & visit all positions. Ammunition carried up by B section to complete each position. Forthcoming raid by 10th Inf Bde cancelled. Enemy Machine Guns more active than usual.	OK
— " —	13/11/17		New H: BRADBURY visits gun positions. 2.15pm CO attend conference at Brigade HQ. Lieut SIM from ARRAS reconnoitres positions in the line.	OK

Army Form C. 2118.

WAR DIARY
or
INTELLIGENCE SUMMARY.
(Erase heading not required.)

Place	Date	Hour	Summary of Events and Information	Remarks and references to Appendices
LINE N.4.b.90.45	12/4/17		Prior to relief on 15th inst. Enemy Machine Guns swept EAST RESERVE at irregular intervals	OR
"	13/4/17		Our Machine Guns fire 21,000 Rds on enemy positions. 6.0 visits positions in the line. 2 Lt J.L. ROGERS proceeds to positions in the line prior to inter-section relief. Orders for inter-section relief issued.	OR
"	14/4/17		Number of rounds fired by our guns 15,000. 6.0 along with Lieut LEASK and Sergt TONNS reconnoitre positions for Strafe taking place on 15th inst. Enemy machine guns fire short bursts on SHRAPNEL, SADDLE & HILL support during the night. 6.0 visits line. Preparations for inter-section reliefs made.	BMR
"	15/4/17	2.0 PM	The # teams of B at Boy HQ proceed to line to relieve D section.	OR
	–"–		The 3 teams of C at ARRAS proceed to the line to relieve A section.	

WAR DIARY
INTELLIGENCE SUMMARY

Place	Date	Hour	Summary of Events and Information	Remarks and references to Appendices
LINE N.45.9.0.4.5	15/4/17	6-0 P.M.	Relief complete by 6-0 p.m. D section after relief come to Coy HQ. 2 teams of A proceed to ARRAS. Lieut MAGUIE + 2 teams of A remain in the line until after raid has taken place, giving barrage fire. Situation normal.	BAR
"	16/4/17		Lieut L.R. Broadhead proceeds to ARRAS. Number of Rds fired by our M.Gs. during night 8,000. Raid takes place at 2-10 A.M. + is carried out successfully. Lieut Maguie + 2 teams A arrive at Coy HQ + proceed to ARRAS. Ammunition carried up to complete each position. Lieut BRADBURY visits all gun positions. Lieut J.R.T LEASK injured by a piece of chalk, + proceeds to Hospital. Lieut E.H. ROSE takes charge of B section in the line.	BAR
"	17/4/17	10.0	Visits all gun positions. Ammunition carried up to positions ready for strafe. Situation fairly quiet.	BAR

Army Form C. 2118.

WAR DIARY
or
INTELLIGENCE SUMMARY.
(Erase heading not required.)

Instructions regarding War Diaries and Intelligence Summaries are contained in F. S. Regs., Part II. and the Staff Manual respectively. Title pages will be prepared in manuscript.

Place	Date	Hour	Summary of Events and Information	Remarks and references to Appendices
LINE N4 b 60 45	18/4/17		Imports taken to position slices of fuse carr out ready for	OMR
		3.0 am	laid on 20th inst. Smoke barrage put on German lines. Machine Guns gave barrage fire. No: of rds fired 8,000	
			Lieut H BRADBURY wounded (shrapnel) transmitted to Hospital.	OMR
"	19/4/17		Guns put in position ready laid for Stafke. Lieut MACVIE proceeds to the line from ARRAS to relieve Lieut ROSE M.G.C. who proceeds to Coy H.Q to take over duties of Second-in-Command. Final Orders for Strafe issued. Enemy Machine Guns active throughout the night.	OMR
"	20/4/17	6.30 am	Raid takes place. 12 of our M.Gs gave barrage fire. No: of Rounds fired during raid 25,000 Rds. Gun teams at Coy H.Q. Carry up S.A.A. to complete each position. A section is withdrawn from the line & proceeds to Billets in ARRAS	OMR

Army Form C. 2118.

WAR DIARY
or
INTELLIGENCE SUMMARY.
(Erase heading not required.)

Instructions regarding War Diaries and Intelligence Summaries are contained in F. S. Regs., Part II. and the Staff Manual respectively. Title pages will be prepared in manuscript.

Place	Date	Hour	Summary of Events and Information	Remarks and references to Appendices
LINE M.4.b.90.45	20/11/17	—	2 Lieut J.L. Rogers temporarily attached 292 Bde R.F.A. Orders issued for 2 Lieut F.P. Muir & F.A. section in ARRAS to proceed to Bay HQ	RWR
— " —	21/11/17	—	Our guns give harassing fire during the night. 2.0. 112 M.G. Coy arrives at Bay HQ to arrange details for relief on 23/11/17. A section under 2 Lieut F.P. Muir arrive at Bay HQ & are installed in dugouts on BROWN LINE Preliminary orders re relief issued. Situation in the line normal.	RWR
— " —	22/11/17	—	C.O. visits all positions in the line. Preparations for relief next day made. Hostile artillery more active than usual. MONCHY & support lines being shelled the most.	RWR
— " —	23/11/17	10 a.m.	C.O. visits Machine Gun positions in 102 Inf Brigade sector.	RWR

A.5834. Wt.W.4973/M687 750,000 8/16 D.D. & L.Ltd. Forms/C.2118/13.

WAR DIARY
INTELLIGENCE SUMMARY

Army Form C. 2118.

Place	Date	Hour	Summary of Events and Information	Remarks and references to Appendices
LINE M 6 b 9 0 4 5	23/4/17	2-0 PM	Relieving company arrive at Bay H.Q. Guides conduct relieving teams to positions. Relief completed by 5-0 P.M. After relief company proceeds - by sections to billets in ARRAS. Hot meal provided for sections on arrival.	JMR
ARRAS			Company H.Q. is established in RUE FREDERIC DEGEORGE. Company parades; Kit Inspection; cleaning of guns + equipment	JMR
"	24/4/17		Company attend Divine Services. Lieut G.V. Foot, 2 Lieuts E.A. Boyce, + A. Abbott + 5 ORs join company from Base.	JMR
"	25/4/17		2 Lieut J.L. Rogers proceeds to Base. Company training during the morning. Baths in the afternoon.	JMR
"	26/4/17		Lieut H. Mauric proceeds to the line to reconnoitre gun positions in 10th Brigade sector	JMR

Army Form C. 2118.

WAR DIARY
or
INTELLIGENCE SUMMARY.
(Erase heading not required.)

Place	Date	Hour	Summary of Events and Information	Remarks and references to Appendices
ARRAS	27/11/17	10 A.M.	C.O. attends conference at H.Q. of 1/Kings Own Regt. Company training carried out. All Box respirators fitted with new containers. Lieut. F Conery proceeds on leave.	SHR
"	28/11/17		C & D Sections parade with 1/Kings Own & 2/Hants.Bns for tactical scheme. Return at 1-45 P.M. Remainder carry out usual Company training	CHR
"	29/11/17		A & B Sections parade with 2/Dukes & 2/Essex for tactical scheme. Remainder of Company proceed through Divisional Gas chamber.	CHR
"	30/11/17		Physical training under Army Gymnastic Instructors. Continuation of Company training.	CHR

Vol 24

CONFIDENTIAL

WAR DIARY

OF

12TH MACHINE GUN COMPANY

(VOLUME XXIV)

FROM 1st December 1917 To 31st December 1917

T.B.Merrick. Lieut
Commanding 12th Machine Gun Company

Army Form C. 2118.

WAR DIARY
or
INTELLIGENCE SUMMARY.
(Erase heading not required.)

Instructions regarding War Diaries and Intelligence Summaries are contained in F. S. Regs., Part II. and the Staff Manual respectively. Title pages will be prepared in manuscript.

Place	Date	Hour	Summary of Events and Information	Remarks and references to Appendices
ARRAS	1/12/17		Company attends Presentation Parade. Medals presented by Major Bonnewier.	T.B.M.
		2.30 P.M.	10 O.R's of 102 M.G Coy HQ in lieu to make arrangements for relief taking place on 3rd.	
"	2/12/17	10-0 AM	Guns & Tripods inspected by Inspector of Armourers. Company attend Divine Service. 3 Section Officers proceed to the line to reconnoitre positions etc.	T.B.M.
"	3/12/17	10-0 AM	Company Operation Order No 20 issued (see appendix A). Section parades and move off to relieve 102 M G Coy.	
line		6.0 PM	B Section take up positions in the intermediate line. Orders issued for D Section in ARRAS to proceed to Company HQ.	T.B.M.
MONCHY Right Sub-Sector	4/12/17	9.0 AM	Relief completed by 2-0 P.M. Situation normal. D Section arrive at Company HQ. 1 Gun placed on Anti-aircraft duties. Remaining 3 Teams stay at SHAMROCK CORNER	T.B.M.

Army Form C. 2118.

WAR DIARY
or
INTELLIGENCE SUMMARY.
(Erase heading not required.)

Place	Date	Hour	Summary of Events and Information	Remarks and references to Appendices
LINE Monchy Right Sub-Sector	4/4/17		C.O. visits all gun positions in the line. Lieut L.R. BROADHEAD returns from leave. Situation in the line fairly quiet.	T.B.M.
	5/4/17		Lieut T.B. MERRICK. M.C. joins Company for duties of second in command. Situation normal.	T.B.M.
	6/4/17		C.O. visits positions in the line. Working party found to construct gun position on CAMBRAI Rd. Situation quiet.	T.B.M.
	7/4/17		Guns in R3 & R4 gave harassing fire during the night firing 4,000 Rds. C.O. visits Brigade H.Q. Situation normal	T.B.M.
	8/4/17		Lieut T.B. MERRICK visits all gun positions. Guns in Int. 1 and 2 gave harassing fire on enemy lines of approach. No. of rounds fired. 4,000	T.B.M.

WAR DIARY
or
INTELLIGENCE SUMMARY

(Erase heading not required.)

Army Form C. 2118.

Instructions regarding War Diaries and Intelligence Summaries are contained in F.S. Regs., Part II. and the Staff Manual respectively. Title pages will be prepared in manuscript.

Place	Date	Hour	Summary of Events and Information	Remarks and references to Appendices
LINE	9/4/17		C.O visits positions in the line. Ammunition supplies placed in M.G. defence positions in the BROWN LINE. Guns in INT. 1 and 2 fire 6,000 Rds during the night. Situation quiet.	7.18.u.
MONCHY Right Sub-Sector	10/4/17		BROWN LINE manned daily from 6-30 AM until Daunion ordered. D section guns are placed in S 3, 4, 5, 6 positions in BROWN LINE. Guns in INT 3 and R 1 & 2 fire 9,000 Rds during the night.	7.8.u.
	11/4/17		Inter section relief carried out D section relieves A section. Relief complete at 1.0 pm. Situation normal.	7.11.u.
	12/4/17 10-0 AM		Conference of C.Os at Brigade HQ. Brent Merrick visits all Gun positions. Situation quiet.	7.10.u.

WAR DIARY
INTELLIGENCE SUMMARY

Army Form C. 2118.

Place	Date	Hour	Summary of Events and Information	Remarks and references to Appendices
LINE	12/2/17	—	Machine Guns in I.3, R.3, & R.4 fired harassing fire during the night. Number of Rounds fired 9,000.	T.K.M.
MONCHY Right sub sector	13/2/17	—	Situation very quiet. Machine Guns in R.3 & R.4 fired 6,000 Rds during the night on enemy lines of approach.	T.K.M.
	14/2/17	—	G.O. visits Bde H.Q. Lieut-Colonel — returns from leave. Situation on the line normal. Guns in R.1 & R.2 fire 4,000 Rds during the night. Situation quiet.	T.K.M.
	15/2/17	1.50 am	Machine Guns fire 13,000 Rds in connection with raid on enemy line. Guns in I.3 & I.4 fire 6,000 Rds on enemy reserve line during the night. 1 O.R. wounded.	T.K.M.
	16/2/17	—	Situation quiet. Machine Guns in R.1 & R.2 fire 6,000 Rds during night.	T.K.M.
	17/2/17	—	Lieut S.I.M. proceeds to U.K. on leave. Machine Guns in I.3 & I.4 fire 6,000 Rds during the night.	T.K.M.

Army Form C. 2118.

WAR DIARY
or
INTELLIGENCE SUMMARY.
(Erase heading not required.)

Instructions regarding War Diaries and Intelligence Summaries are contained in F. S. Regs., Part II. and the Staff Manual respectively. Title pages will be prepared in manuscript.

Place	Date	Hour	Summary of Events and Information	Remarks and references to Appendices
LINE MONCHY Right Sub-Sector	19/4/17		Situation quiet. O.C. 112th M.G. Coy visits Company HQ to arrange details of relief.	T.B.M.
			Company Operation Order No 21 issued.	see appendix "B"
			Guns on R1 & R2 fire 4,000 Rds during the night.	
	20/4/17		Company relieved by 112th M.G. Company. Relief complete by 4.0 p.m. Company after relief proceed to billets in ARRAS.	T.B.M.
ARRAS	21/4/17		Company training carried out. Firing practice on MOAT Range.	T.B.M.
"	22/4/17	6.30 A.M	Company "Stand to".	
			Company cleaning & guns & personal equipment.	T.B.M
			O.C. attend conference at Bde H.Q.	
"	23/4/17	6.30 A.M	Company "Stand to".	T.B.M
"	23/4/17	9.45 A.M	Company inspected by G.O.C. 12th Inf. Brigade.	T.B.M
"	24/4/17		Company attend Divine Services.	T.B.M

Boismont

Army Form C. 2118.

WAR DIARY
or
INTELLIGENCE SUMMARY
(Erase heading not required.)

Instructions regarding War Diaries and Intelligence Summaries are contained in F. S. Regs., Part II. and the Staff Manual respectively. Title pages will be prepared in manuscript.

Place	Date	Hour	Summary of Events and Information	Remarks and references to Appendices
ARRAS	25/10/17		Company holds its previous positions	T.B.M.
"	26/10/17		C.O.s conference at Bde H.Q.	T.B.M.
"			C.O. & Section Officers reconnoitre positions in the line	See appendix C
LINE	27/10/17		Company Operation Orders No 22 issued	T.B.M.
MDH CA/			Company relieve 102 M.G. Coy in the line.	
Left sub Sector			Relief complete by 3-0 P.M.	
			Situation quiet	
"	28/10/17		C.O. visits all gun positions in the line	T.A.M.
			Situation normal.	
			Machine Guns in I9, R8, R9 fire 6,000 Rds during the night	
"	29/10/17		Lieut Merrick M.C. visits all positions, situation normal.	T.B.M.
			Guns in R5 & R6 fire 6,000 Rds during the night on enemy lines of approach.	
			Situation quiet. Guns in R15 & R14 fire 4,000 Rds	T.B.M.
	30/10/17		C.O. proceeds to Transport lines	T.B.M.
	31/10/17		Situation normal.	

APPENDIX "A"

SECRET.   COPY No. 10

No. 12 Machine Gun Company Operation Order No. 20.
_____

Reference Sheet 51B N.W. & 51B S.W. 1/20,000

                                                          1st DECEMBER 1917.

1. The 12th Machine Gun Company will relieve the 10th Machine Gun Company on the morning of the 3rd inst.

2. Nos 1, 2, 3, & 4 Teams of A Section under Lieut. MACVIE and 2/Lieut. MUTCH will take over positions numbered S 1, S 2, S 3, & S 4 respectively.

3. Nos 5, 6, 7, and 8 Teams of B Section under 2/Lieut ARLETT will take over positions numbered R 1, R 2, R 3, and R 4.

4. Nos 9, 10, and 11 Teams of C Section under Lieut. SIM will be in Reserve at SHAMROCK CORNER, No 12 Team will take over the A.A. position at Company H.Q.

5. D Section under 2/Lieut. BOYCE will remain in ARRAS. Billets will be notified later.

6. Sections will march off from Billets at 9-00 a.m., a distance of 200 yards being kept between Sections. H.Q. will march off at 9-30 a.m.

7. One Limber will be required for each Section. Limbers should be at Billet in BOULEVARD CARNOT at 8-30 a.m.

8. One Limber for H.Q. will be at Orderly Room at 9-00 a.m.

9. Guides will be met at Company H.Q.

10. Guns, Tripods, Spare Parts and Clinometers will be taken up.

11. All maps, trench stores, water tins, etc, will be taken over.

12. Bolt Boxes will be taken over by A & B Sections. C Section will take up 14 boxes per Team.

13. Lists of all stores taken over will be forwarded to Company H.Q.

14. Acknowledge.

                                                CHRoxx   Lieut,
Issued at 8-00 p.m.   A/Adjt No. 12 Machine Gun Company.
Distribution:-
   Copies Nos 1 to 6 Officers.
             7. C.S.M.
             8. C.Q.M.S.
             9. War Diary.
            10. File.

APPENDIX "B"

SECRET   COPY No. 10

No. 12 Machine Gun Company Operation Order No. 21.

Ref: Sheet 51B N.W., & 51B S.W. 1/40,000.   18th DECEMBER 1917

1. The 12th Machine Gun Company will be relieved by the 11th Machine Gun Company on the morning of the 19th inst.

2. Guide for S 1, guide for S 2 and S 3, and guide for S 4 will be ready at Company H.Q. at 11-30 a.m.

3. Two guides for R 1, 2, 3, and 4 will be ready at Company H.Q. at 11-45 a.m.

4. Guide for Int: 1 and 2, and guide for Int: 3 and 4 will be ready at Company H.Q. at 12-0 noon.

5. A guide will be at junction of track and BILLON Rd at 11-00 a.m.

6. All guides will be supplied by personnel at Company H.Q.

7. All belt boxes, maps, trench stores, etc, will be handed over and a complete list handed in to Company H.Q. on relief.

8. All teams will report to Company H.Q. on relief.

9. Every position and dug-out will be left in a perfectly clean condition.

10. All water tins will be left full.

11. The Transport Officer will arrange for two limbers to be at Company H.Q. at 12-30 p.m. and two at 1-30 p.m.

12. The C.Q.M.S. will meet the Section at billets and will arrange for a hot meal to be ready

13. Acknowledge.

                                    (signature) Capt.
                                    A/Capt. No. 12 Machine Gun Company.

Issued at 3-00 p.m.
  Distribution:-   Copy No. 1   Lieut. ROSE.M.G.   Copy No. 7 C.S.M.
                        "   2   "   FOX   8 O.MS.
                        "   3   "   MacIVER   9 Files.
                        "   4   2/Lieut. ABBERT   10 War
                        "   5   "   " BOYCE   diary.
                        "   6   "   " HUTCH.

APPENDIX "C"

SECRET   C O P Y no......12....

12th Machine Gun Company Operation Order No. 22.

Ref: Sheets 51B N.W. & 51B S.W. 1/20,000.   26th DECEMBER 1917

1. The 12th Machine Gun Company will relieve the 10th Machine Gun Company in the Left Sector on the morning of the 27th inst.

2. Nos: 1, 2, 3, & 4 teams of A Section under Lieut. N. MAGVIE and 2:Lieut. F.P.MUTCH will relieve positions numbered R 5, R 6, R 8, R9 respectively.

3. Nos: 5, 6, 7, & 8 teams of B Section under Lieut. F. COMERY and 2/Lieut. A. ABLETT will relieve positions numbered S 5, R 14, R 16, & Int 9 respectively.

4. Nos: 13, 14, 15, & 16 teams of D Section under Lieut E.N.ROSE.M.C. & 2/Lieut. L.R.BROADHEAD will relieve positions numbered R 12, R13, R 15, & R 17 respectively

5. C Section under 2/Lieut. E.A.BOYCE will be in reserve at Company H.Q.

6. Times for leaving billets will be as follows:-

Teams	Position No.	Time
No. 1.	R 5.)	
" 2.	~~R 6.~~) R 8	
" 3.	~~R 8.~~) R 9	10-15 a.m.
" 4.	~~R 9.~~) R 6	
" 5.	~~S 5.~~) R 16	
" 6.	~~R 14.~~) I 9	10-30 a.m.
" 7.	~~R 16.~~) S 5	
" 8.	~~Int 9~~) R 14	
" 13.	~~R 12.~~) R 15	
" 14.	~~R 13.~~) R 12	10-00 a.m.
" 15.	~~R 15.~~) R 13	
" 16.	R 17.)	

Company H.Q.   10-45 a.m.

C Section.   12-00 noon.

7. One limber will be required for each Section and one for Company H.Q. The Transport Officer will arrange for limbers to be at billets 10 minutes before each party starts.

8. Each party will halt for 10 minutes after one hours marching.

9. Guides will be met at Company H.Q.

10. Bolt boxes, magzs, trench stores, etc will be taken over, a list of everything taken over at each position being forwarded to Company H.Q.

11. All billets will be thoroughly cleaned before being vacated. C Section will finally clean up after the remaining Sections have left.

12. Billets for Q.M. Stores and details will be notified later.

13. Acknowledge.

          C.B.Mennick
                   Lieut,
         A/Adjt No. 18 Machine Gun Company.

Issued at

Distribution:- Copies No. 1 to 8 Officers.
            9. C.S.M.
           10. C.Q.M.S.
           11. File.
           12. War diary.

4th Division

12th M. G. C.

January 1918

W.M 25

CONFIDENTIAL

WAR DIARY

OF

12TH MACHINE GUN COMPANY

(VOLUME XXV)

FROM 1st January 1918 To 31st January 1918

T.B. Warrick. M.T. Captain

Commanding 12th Machine Gun Company

31/1/1918

Army Form C. 2118.

WAR DIARY
~~INTELLIGENCE SUMMARY.~~
(Erase heading not required.)

Place	Date	Hour	Summary of Events and Information	Remarks and references to Appendices
LINE MONCHY	1/1/1918	—	Situation in the line normal. Lieut H Marris proceeded on leave. M.G.s in R 14 & R 15 fire 4,000 Rds during the night on enemy supports	BHR
LEFT SUB-SECTOR	2/1/1918	—	Lieut Merrick M.C. visits positions in the line. Situation quiet. M.G.s in R.8. & R.9 fire 4000 Rds during the night	CHR
"	3/1/1918	—	Situation normal. M.G.s in I 9 & R 15. fire 6,000 Rds on enemy lines of approach during the night	CHR
"	4/1/1918	—	Captain Bennett rejoins from R.F.C. M.G.s in R.14 & R.8 fire 6,000 Rds.	CHR
"	5/1/1918	—	C.O. visits all gun positions. Situation quiet. M.G.s in R 9 & R 15 fire 4,000 Rds on enemy tracks	CHR
"	6/1/18	—	C.O's conference at Bde H.Q. 2 Guns of B dicken moved from BROWN LINE to positions in HAPPY VALLEY. M.G.s in I 9 & R 8. fire 4000 Rds during the night.	CHR
"	7/1/18	—	C.O visits positions in the line. Situation normal. M.G.s in R 8 & R 14 fire 4,000 Rds during the night.	CHR
"	8/1/18	—	Situation normal. Lieut Merrick visits gun positions	CHR
"	9/1/18	—	Situation quiet. C.O visits all gun positions	CHR

Army Form C. 2118.

WAR DIARY
or
INTELLIGENCE SUMMARY.
(Erase heading not required.)

Instructions regarding War Diaries and Intelligence Summaries are contained in F.S. Regs., Part II. and the Staff Manual respectively. Title pages will be prepared in manuscript.

Place	Date	Hour	Summary of Events and Information	Remarks and references to Appendices
LINE MONCHY LEFT SUB-SECTOR	10/1/1918		New M.G. positions taken over. No visits all positions M G's in R5, R6, & R14 fire 7,000 Rds during the night. Situation normal.	TWM
	11/1/18		Company Operation Orders for relief taking place on 12th inst issued Officer Commanding relieving Company visits Bn HQ	TWM See Appendix
	12/1/18	11-0 AM	Company relieved in the line by the 112 M.G. Coy. Relief complete by 3-0 P.M. After relief Company proceed to	A TWM
BOIS-DES-BOEUFFS	13/1/18		BOIS-DES-BOEUFFS Camp. Company Operation Orders for field firing scheme issued Company taking parade	TWM
		2-0 P.M.	60 proceeds on leave to UK. Field firing scheme cancelled.	
	14/1/18		Cleaning guns equipment etc. Sections carry on work	TWM
	15/1/18		Company training carried out.	TWM
	16/1/18		Company training as usual. G.O.C. 12th Inf. Brigade visits Camp & inspects Coy Billets	TWM
	17/1/18		Cleaning of guns equipment etc.	TWM
	18/1/18	10-20 AM	Inspection of Company by G.O.C. Brigade & D.M.G.O. Inspection takes place in the huts.	TWM

Army Form C. 2118.

WAR DIARY
or
INTELLIGENCE SUMMARY.
(Erase heading not required.)

Instructions regarding War Diaries and Intelligence Summaries are contained in F. S. Regs., Part II. and the Staff Manual respectively. Title pages will be prepared in manuscript.

Place	Date	Hour	Summary of Events and Information	Remarks and references to Appendices
BOIS-DES-BOEUFFS	19/1/1918		Lieut MERRICK. M.C. visits 102 M.G. Coy H.Q to arrange details of relief taking place on 20th inst.	T.B.M.
"	20/1/918		Company Operation Order No 25 issued. Company relieves 102 M.G Coy in the line. Relief complete by 2-30 P.M. Situation Normal.	See appendix B T.B.M.
LINE MOMCHY RIGHT SUB-SECTOR	21/1/18		Lieut Merrick M.C visits all Gun Positions. Situation quiet	T.B.M.
"	22/1/18		Situation normal. L.O visits all positions. Enemy M.G's fire intermittently during the night	T.B.M.
"	23/1/18		L.O visits all positions. Situation quiet.	T.B.M.
"	24/1/18		Situation on the line normal.	T.B.M.
"	25/1/18		L.O visits all Gun positions. Enemy M.G's fire bursts during the night	T.B.M.
"	26/1/18		Situation normal	T.B.M.
"	27/1/18		Machine Guns in R.3 R.8 fire 5000 Rds on enemys tracks etc. L.O visits all positions. Situation Normal	T.B.M.

Army Form C. 2118.

WAR DIARY
or
INTELLIGENCE SUMMARY.
(Erase heading not required.)

Instructions regarding War Diaries and Intelligence Summaries are contained in F. S. Regs., Part II. and the Staff Manual respectively. Title pages will be prepared in manuscript.

Place	Date	Hour	Summary of Events and Information	Remarks and references to Appendices
LINE MONCHY	29/1/18		Situation in the line normal. Enemy artillery active during the night.	T.W.M.
RIGHT SUB-SECTOR	30/1/18		Lieut Merrick M.C. took all gun positions. M.G. in R.9 fired 2,000 Rds during the night. Captain Burnett rejoins from leave.	T.W.M.
"	30/1/18		B.O visits all gun positions.	T.W.M.
"	31/1/18		Situation normal. M.G. in R.3. position fired 2,000 Rds during the night on the reverse slope of the MOUND. Situation in the line quiet. M.G. in R.8 position fired 2,000 Rds on sunken slope Bois de VERT. O.O visits all positions	T.W.M.

APPENDIX "A"

SECRET.   COPY No..............

18th Machine Gun Company Operation Order No. 25.

Ref: Sheet 51B N.W. & 51B S.W. 1/20,000.   10th JANUARY, 1918

1. The 18th Machine Gun Company will relieve the 20th M.G. Company in the ~~Left~~ RIGHT Sub-Sector on the morning of the 10th inst.

2. DETAILS OF RELIEF:-

   Company H.Q. leaves at 11-00 a.m.

   #### B Section
		Time of
Lieut. F. COMERY	"B" Strong Point.	departure
2/Lieut. A. SMYTH.	B 8 Position	
No. 5 Team.	B 1 "	
" 6. "	B 7 "	
" 7. "	B 8 "	10-00 a.m.
" 8. "	B 9 "	

   #### D Section.
2/Lieut. L.E. BROADMEAD.	D 3 Position.	
No. 23 Team.	D 5 "	
" 14 "	D 4 "	10-15 a.m.
" 16 "	D 3 "	

   #### C Section.
1/Lieut. E.A. BOYCE.	"B" Strong Point.	
No. 9 Team.	I 1 Position.	
" 10. "	I 3 "	10-30 a.m.
" 11. "	I 2 "	
" 12. "	I 4. "	

   #### A Section
Lieut. G.E. UN.	Company H.Q.	
No. 1 Team.	A 5 Position	
" 2 "	A 6 "	10-45 AM
" 3 "	A 1 "	
" 4 "	A 3 "	
" 15 "	A 5 " (Corps Line)	

3. GUIDES:- One guide per team will be at junction of CORPS LINE and CAMBRAI ROAD. First Section at 11-00 a.m., other Sections at ½ hour intervals.

4. LIMBERS:- One Limber per Section, and two for H.Q. will report at Company Billet 30 minutes before times allotted for departure.

5. Belt boxes will be taken over. Lists of trench stores taken over to be sent to Company H.Q. immediately after relief.

6. Rations will be issued at 9-00 a.m. in bulk to Sections

7. Section Officers will report to Company H.Q. ½ of an hour before departure that huts are absolutely clean

8. Acknowledge.

P H Rice Lieut,

A/Adjt 10th Machine Gun Company.

Issued at 6-00 p.m.

Distribution:-   Copy No. 1. Lieut. COMBY
                          2.   "   SIM.
                          3.   "   COX.
                          4. 2/Lieut. BROADHEAD.
                          5.   "   WILLETT.
                          6.   "   BOYCE.
                          7. O.R.R.
                          8. C.Q.M.S.
                          9. File.
                         10. WAR DIARY.
                         11. "   "

APPENDIX 'B'

SECRET   COPY No. 11

18th Machine Gun Company Operation Order No. 98

Reference Sheet 51 B N.W. & 51B S.W. 1/20,000.   11th JANUARY 1917.

1. The 18th Machine Gun Company will be relieved by the 21th Machine Gun Company on the morning of the 12th inst.

2. One guide will be sent to Coy H.Q. from each position.

3. All above guides will be at Coy H.Q. by 11 a.m.

4. All teams will report to Coy H.Q. on relief.

5. All belt boxes, maps, water tins, trench stores etc, will be handed over on relief, and a complete list handed in to Company H.Q.

6. Every Gun position and dug-out will be handed over in a perfectly clean condition and a certificate obtained from relieving Officer to this effect.

7. All water tins will be left full.

8. The Transport Officer will arrange for one limber to be at Company H.Q. at each of the following times:-

    11.30 A.M.   12.30 P.M.   2 P.M.

9. On relief Sections will march to Camp at BOIS DES BOEUFS

10. C.Q.M.S. will arrange for a hot meal to be ready at:-
    3 P.M.

11. Acknowledge.

                                T.B.Merrick   Lieut,
Issued at 9-00 p.m.   A/Adjt 18th Machine Gun Company.

Distribution:-

     Copy No. 1 Lieut. ROSE.M.C,
          "   2   "   O'MERY.
          "   3   "   SIM.
          "   4   "   FOX.
          "   5 2/Lieut. BROADHEAD.
          "   6   "   BOYCE
          "   7 C.S.M.
          "   8 C.Q.M.S.
          "   9 FILE
          " 10. & 11 War Diary.

www.ingramcontent.com/pod-product-compliance
Lightning Source LLC
Chambersburg PA
CBHW080846230426
43662CB00013B/2038